God Moments

101 Little Lessons for Life's Journey

Jo-Anne Berthelsen

Authentic

First published 2024 by Authentic Media Limited,
PO Box 6326, Bletchley, Milton Keynes, MK1 9GG.
authenticmedia.co.uk

British Library Cataloguing in Publication Data
A catalogue record for this book is available from the British Library.
ISBN: 978-1-78893-383-4
978-1-78893-384-1 (e-book)

Cover design by Claire Marshall

In the maelstrom that is modern living, we too rarely take opportunities to pause and reflect. As a result, we regularly fail to hear or notice the still small voice of God speaking through events in our daily lives. Jo-Anne Berthelsen adopts an alternative posture. In this book she invites the reader to slow down, look, notice and reflect. Drawing upon vignettes from her own experiences, she offers us 'little lessons for life's journey'. Here are simple, applicable lessons, distilled by prayerful reflection on diverse, often overlooked daily events. They are lessons to encourage, support and grow those who take a few moments to pause, be still and listen for the God of all grace. One of the charms of the book is that it models for the reader a way of reflecting on the mundane so that God's voice is clearer and his lessons able to be internalised. The volume helpfully categorises the 'lessons' under ten themes, while thoughtful headings for each reflection invite curiosity about what is to follow. As Jo-Anne comments, 'In all these situations, we need to have our ears attuned to that still, small voice of the Spirit.' This little work can assist you to do just that! Work through it sequentially or dip into randomly: either way it will reward you.

Revd Dr Viv Grice, Baptist pastor, professional supervisor (pastoral)

Jo-Anne Berthelsen has a gift of noticing the little things that most of us miss. In this book of short reflections, she makes connections between seemingly insignificant, everyday happenings and the sort of practical wisdom that reflects God's character. Read this a little at a time and be inspired to pay attention to the lessons that come through the details of life.

Dr Rick Lewis, mentor, trainer, church consultant, author of Mentoring Matters *https://anamcaraconsulting.com.au/*

Jo-Anne writes with a depth of honesty, displaying true empathy. Her practical wisdom, insight and godly perspective always serve to encourage me. She takes simple, everyday encounters and experiences and transforms them into lessons of grace.

Michelle Dona, English tutor

I first met Jo-Anne when she spoke at our church's Ladies' Fellowship and her words went straight to my writer's heart. Discovering her blogs was like meeting with her regularly, receiving the encouragement, wisdom and humour she so generously shares. Her reflections conduct us through her life and ours as we journey together in the light of God's love and demonstrate how he is always there, in life's big picture and minutiae. They remind us of his goodness, and lift our hearts and souls.

Dr Jeanie Wood, teacher and author of The Travel Club *novels,* Finding Joy *and* The Heart Has Many Rooms

Often, the life we see before us is so ordinary. Jo-Anne captures so beautifully a second glance through the lens of our God, the Creator. Inspiring!

Lyndon Rumsey, pastor

If you want to see God in your everyday life, then this is the book for you. In short stories from her own life, Jo-Anne takes the exploits and conversations with her grandchildren, her unexpected encounters with strangers, the mundane activities of cooking, gardening and just about everything else in her life to show us God's character and the way he speaks in the ordinary and extraordinary events she experiences every day. She combines her deep knowledge of the Bible with the everyday aspects of life and encourages us to experience God in our own lives too.

Marjan Beer, pastor (retired), mentor

This beautifully authored collection of life-giving stories highlights the powerful influence of pondering on the 'God incidents' in our day-to-day lives. Jo-Anne writes with gentle transparency, and reading her book is like delving into a treasure chest, with each story unveiling another gem from the depths of her soul. As I read, my heart resonated with joy as her contemplative words ministered deeply, drawing me into a place of meaningful insight and reflection on similar stories in my own life. Jo-Anne's ultimate desire is that 'we would learn to value our close connection with God so much more and truly cherish his loving intimate presence each day'.

Jenni Gainer, Spiritual Mentor

Other books by Jo-Anne Berthelsen

Swansong: Start Creating Your Legacy of Life-Giving Words Today

Dedication

To our awesome Lord God, who has patiently persevered in teaching and encouraging me throughout my life. May I continue to listen to your voice and learn to follow you even more closely, day by day.

Take my yoke upon you and learn from me, for I am gentle and humble in heart, and you will find rest for your souls.
Matthew 11:29

Acknowledgements

To all the faithful readers of my weekly blogs over many years, especially to those who encouraged me to compile a similar volume of short pieces of writing as I have now done, a heartfelt thank you.

To my publishers, Authentic Media UK, and the wonderful team there – Donna, Claire, Roxanne and Rachael – heartfelt thanks for all your warm encouragement, careful editing and promotional efforts on my behalf.

To those who have graciously taken the time to write endorsements for *God Moments: 101 Little Lessons for Life's Journey* – Viv Grice, Rick Lewis, Michelle Dona, Jeanie Wood, Lyndon Rumsey, Marjan Beer and Jenni Gainer – thank you so much. I appreciate you all.

To my husband, Lionel, thank you for your ongoing help with all things technical and financial to do with my books, and for your encouragement and belief in me down through the years.

Last but by no means least, to my email prayer team – Ruth A, Marjan, Michelle, Liz, Judy M, Kerry, Joan, Judy S, Ruth S and Rhondda – thank you so much for all your faithful support throughout my writing and speaking journey.

Contents

Introduction

Whoever we are and whatever our life situation, we all wake up in the morning with so many possibilities awaiting us. What will we see or hear today? What will we read somewhere? Who will we talk to? What thoughts and memories will stir in our minds and hearts? What does God have to show us or teach us?

Often, I am asked how I can keep writing my books and weekly blogs. Where do I get all my ideas from? How can I think of new and different things to say? Each time, I am genuinely amazed at these questions because, to me, everywhere I look, there are stories that need to be told and fascinating people and things crying out to be noticed. On top of that, each day as I read God's word and listen to God's Spirit, I find some fresh encouragement or challenge or insight that I long to pass on to others in some shape or form. To me, the possibilities each day contains are endless.

As I grow older, the possibilities of learning new things or of being reminded of old things I may have forgotten seem endless too. Everywhere around us, there are still lessons waiting to be learned and wisdom to be welcomed into our hearts. In our lifetime, we merely scratch the surface of all there is to know about our wonderful world – and all there is to know about God and how we are called to live out our days here. What a joy then to keep on learning and gaining wisdom – and what a joy to keep on growing closer to God, listening well to the Spirit's promptings and acting upon them.

In this volume, I have included a selection of little lessons that have touched my heart, mind and soul in some significant way, drawn me closer to God and shown me how to serve others better in my daily life. May they stir your heart, mind and soul too and encourage you as you continue on your own unique life journey, hand in hand with the One who loves you and watches over you with the most amazing, endless mercy and grace.

We Matter

Recently, a friend and I spent time in a meeting with a man who suffers from significant health issues. He shuffles along, using a walker, and appears older than his actual age. He cannot hold things well, often dropping his belongings. He constantly jerks his body from side to side. His eyes cannot seem to focus anywhere for long and he has trouble speaking clearly. As we chatted, he attempted to communicate with my friend and me as best he could, and we tried our hardest to understand and connect with him in return. However, my friend is quite deaf, so it was doubly difficult for her to understand the man's soft, slurred speech. In the end, it was up to me to listen closely, try to grasp the kernel of what the man wanted to say, then relay it to my friend as accurately as possible.

I felt so responsible in undertaking this task. I could tell my friend felt embarrassed that she could not understand so I did what I could to make the whole experience easier for her. But I certainly did not want to short-change the gentleman seated with us either, because I could see how much his desire to engage with us mattered to him. He had important things to share with us about his abilities and career achievements, and wanted to offer his services in these areas in whatever way he could to help out his new community. I could see he had – and has – so much still to give to others. Yet his health challenges make things so difficult for him.

I honour this man for his courage in continuing to strive to reach out and do things. He is definitely not sitting around moping and feeling sorry for himself, as far as I can tell. Yet he cannot now do all those wonderful things he used to love doing – or at least not to the same degree – and I am sure he knows that. So where does he fit now? How can we help him? Even though

this man had difficulty looking directly at me as we chatted, I caught a glimpse in his eyes of his need to be taken seriously, to be listened to, to be respected for all he could offer – in other words, to *matter* to others.

This is such a key issue for us all, isn't it? We want to know that we have some sort of significance in this world, that our being here makes a difference to others in some way. At times, we look in the wrong places for this – and, as has happened with this man, we may be forced to lay aside, either temporarily or permanently, those things we have relied on for our significance. How important it is then to know we truly matter to God, that it is God who gives us significance deep inside ourselves, whatever is happening to and around us. This is the truth that blew me away as a 15-year-old when I committed my life to God – and this is still the truth that sustains me today.

We matter so much to God. May we remember that well.

This is how God showed his love among us: he sent his one and only Son into the world that we might live through him.

1 John 4:9

On God's Love and Grace

Lost

'We're going the long way – we'll still beat you to the car,' our two youngest grandchildren informed us as we went to drive them home after a happy day together. We thought they would try their usual trick of heading upstairs in our unit block, then along and down again, while we took the direct route but, instead, they went further afield. Soon, to their dismay, they became totally lost.

We waited and waited – but no children showed up. I scoured our unit block several times, calling their names. Nothing. I raced up to our village centre. Nothing. I asked others along the way and, while one lady had seen them dash past, there was now no sign of them. Then my husband drove around looking. Again, nothing.

What to do? I stood at a nearby corner, hoping they would see me, and thought of calling the police. But at last, a lady came walking towards me, holding our grandchildren's hands. At that point, she seemed like an angel to me.

'Would you like two grandchildren?' she asked, as I heaved a sigh of relief and tried not to burst into tears.

Our grandchildren looked sober and scared, especially when they saw they had upset me. They explained how they had tried to find their way back but had become completely confused, and their rescuer also explained how our grandson had been very sensible and asked her nicely where our unit was. But what a fright for them – and us! Next time they were with us, they willingly made thank-you cards and some chocolate brownies for their rescuing angel and delivered them to her.

On God's Love and Grace

I wonder if you have had a similar, heart-in-mouth experience of losing someone or of being lost yourself? Once when travelling in Turkey with a friend, I went to find a bank while she waited at the bus station. On the way back, I took a wrong turn and became lost. What to do? With minimal Turkish at my disposal, I somehow managed to ask for directions in a nearby shop but could not understand the information I was given. Eventually, with the help of a stern Turkish policeman, I was reunited with my friend just before our bus arrived. Phew!

We can feel so helpless in such situations, can't we? But these experiences can also teach us something more about God, I believe. Through being lost in Turkey, I realised again my deep need of a rescuer, both then and in my life in general. Without God, we truly are lost, without hope and without purpose in life. Then through losing our grandchildren, even for only a short while, I sensed again God's deep grief when we lose our way in life or reject God's offer of rescue and reconciliation. Yet how eagerly our loving Father waits to welcome us home, just as the father in the story in Luke 15 welcomed his lost son home: 'Bring the fattened calf and kill it. Let's have a feast and celebrate. For this son of mine was dead and is alive again; he was lost and is found' (Luke 15:23–4).

It is never pleasant to be lost – but it is the most wonderful experience ever when we find ourselves back in the loving arms of God, who always delights to welcome us home.

On God's Love and Grace

This I Know

Have you ever witnessed an occasion when some basic truth you and I may feel is far too obvious to bother telling anyone ends up having the most profound impact on a person's life? This can be an important, humbling lesson indeed to learn – and one I hope I never forget.

One evening, I had just finished speaking somewhere when, in response to a question, I decided to share a true story from many years ago with my audience. The women present had all patiently listened to my input, but their noticeably heartfelt reaction to the story I went on to tell them opened my eyes again to the simple yet life-changing truth it contains.

The particular event I shared with them occurred during a ministry training course I attended. Our designated small group was made up of five women, including our facilitator, Joy, who counselled us with gentle wisdom and insight. As we took turns to share any difficulties we were experiencing in applying the course content in our lives, Joy listened carefully – to us and to God. This was never more obvious than when one group member shared how she had never felt loved as a child, particularly by her father, and how much that had affected her throughout her life, especially in regard to her relationship with God.

I cannot recall the conversation that unfolded at that point but I clearly remember what our facilitator decided to do next. Suddenly, Joy moved across to the person who had shared these words, put her arms around her and began singing:

Jesus loves me! This I know,
For the Bible tells me so.

On God's Love and Grace

Little ones to him belong;
They are weak, but he is strong.
Yes, Jesus loves me!
Yes, Jesus loves me!
Yes, Jesus loves me!
The Bible tells me so.[1]

At first, I thought this was a strange and even embarrassing thing to do. However, I soon changed my mind because, whenever Joy stopped singing, the person she was ministering to would exclaim: 'Oh, that's *wonderful – please* sing it again!'

Eventually, Joy asked us all to join in, so we gathered around the two of them and did just that. I will never forget the ecstatic tone in the woman's voice as she begged us to keep singing, and the joy that radiated from her as we did. Her face seemed to shine as the Holy Spirit began pouring God's fatherly love into her, bringing such healing and peace to her heart in the process. Even now, years later, she still clearly remembers this event and smiles almost in ecstasy.

When I recounted this story to my audience that evening, I expected to see some puzzled expressions on their faces. After all, what I described *was* rather unusual. To my surprise, however, I heard what sounded like a soft, collective sigh spread across the entire room. Most responded with warm smiles – and many seemed deeply moved. At that point, I realised this story had in fact been the most significant part of my entire input that evening. Just a simple truth God had prompted me to share, yet it was the very truth these women too needed to hear.

Jesus loves me – this I know. Jesus loves *you* – this I know.

We love because he first loved us.

1 John 4:19

On God's Love and Grace

Learning a New Skill

I am a rather independent person, to say the least. I do not like to admit, even to myself, that I need any sort of help – and I certainly do not like asking for it because I always fear I may inconvenience those around me. Yet it is something I had to learn to do at one stage some years ago, after having a back operation.

While in hospital, I felt so blessed by the gracious way the doctors and nurses attended to my every need. I recall with thankfulness how my kind neurosurgeon came to explain everything clearly to me prior to my operation. I remember the nurse's patient efforts to make me comfortable that first difficult night after surgery. I am so grateful for the one who helped me take my first shower and for the kind physio who walked slowly beside me as I took my first steps down the hallway. All the while, I was learning a new skill – that of humbly receiving help.

At home, I continued to learn slowly. I soon realised the folly of trying to get up from our low sofa without calling on my husband for help. I had to admit I could not possibly change that dressing in the middle of my back without his assistance either. I had to become reconciled to giving him simple cooking instructions and watching him stumble through unknown culinary territory, without trying to get up and make those meals myself. I had to learn to accept wonderful casseroles from a loving daughter who was so tired herself as she neared the birth of her baby. And I knew I needed to accept with grace that bag of goodies left on our doorstep by a friend already dealing with very ill family members of her own at home.

On God's Love and Grace

Gradually, I came to realise what God wanted to teach me. I began to allow others to do their job and not to intervene myself. I began to learn to show gratitude for their servant hearts and to value who they are more fully. I began to receive that love others wanted to show me as they ministered to my needs. I began to learn to ask for help more readily, knowing this does not make me any less of a person and realising this may in fact bless those offering to assist.

Then it dawned on me that I was learning something about my relationship with God through all this as well. It is God's heart desire to care for me – and God's heart is indeed full of perfect love, compassion, patience and comfort. As my loving Father, God sees my every need and delights to use all sorts of means to provide for me. What a huge lesson it was for me to learn all over again to receive from God's gracious hand as I opened my heart more fully to all the wonderful healing mercy others were showing me.

May you too learn to be at peace as you receive whatever help you need from our loving God, above all, but also from those around you.

Yet the LORD longs to be gracious to you;
    therefore he will rise up to show you compassion.
For the LORD is a God of justice.
    Blessed are all who wait for him!

Isaiah 30:18

On God's Love and Grace

Letter of Love

It was a beautiful, sunny day – too beautiful to spend at my desk. So I decided I would potter in our garden for a while instead and pull out some weeds around our letterbox. As I did, I reflected on how little personal mail we now receive. I remembered how, when our children were young and we lived interstate, I would pounce on letters from family members far away and relish reading them. I recalled in particular my mother's letters, written in her rounded handwriting on both sides of small, lined sheets of paper, and I sighed a little. No internet back then or mobile phones for those quick texts back and forth. In fact, in those days, we did not even have a landline in our home.

Gradually, I surfaced from my reminiscences of years ago. What was I doing, standing there on such a beautiful day, wasting time and feeling so nostalgic? At that point, I realised I had not actually checked our letterbox for some time. I reached inside – and there was a thin letter, addressed in handwriting I did not immediately recognise. Perhaps it was from someone wanting to order one of my books, I decided, as I tucked the letter in my pocket and continued weeding.

Eventually, I went inside and opened it. It was from our son, written in gold on black paper – a thank-you letter, putting into words various things he appreciated about our relationship and the way he had been brought up. So many loving comments, written simply and clearly in his own unique way. I reread his words several times, allowing them to sink in and touch my heart. The tears welled up, but not from sadness. Instead, I was filled with joy and gratitude at such an unexpected, affirming gift.

On God's Love and Grace

I sit here now, perusing our son's letter once again. Over the years, our daughters too have expressed similar thoughts, face to face or via email, as they have thanked me for my ongoing support and efforts on their behalf. Of course, I would never think of doing anything less than my best for our children – yet it is so heart-warming to be thanked.

Then I glance out of my window at the deep blue sky and the trees bending in the breeze and realise how often I overlook expressing my own heartfelt thanks to God, not only for the beauty of this world but for everything else I have been given in life. I know God loves me unconditionally. I know God has rescued me. I know God walks with me each day. I have experienced so much of God's grace and goodness. Yet how often do I take it all for granted, as if it was somehow my right, rather than receive it as a wonderful gift?

So now, Lord, I choose to remember all your loving-kindness towards me. My words may seem inadequate and trite, but my heart overflows with deep thankfulness to you. You are a great and awesome God, so worthy of all praise and honour – and I love you with all my heart, soul, mind and strength.

Come, let us sing for joy to the LORD;
   let us shout aloud to the Rock of our salvation.
Let us come before him with thanksgiving
   and extol him with music and song.

Psalm 95:1–2

On God's Love and Grace

A Glimpse of Grace

One birthday, I received a very special gift – a voucher from our daughter and her husband for a restaurant I had always wanted to try but felt was beyond our budget. They could ill afford such an expensive present, yet I knew they gave it in love and wanted my husband and me to enjoy the whole experience.

I made a booking and looked forward to our dinner out with great anticipation, studying the menu online beforehand and deciding how best to use every last cent of that voucher. We also hoped we would do our special meal justice – we had never tasted some of the more exotic items on offer.

When we arrived, we were escorted to a table overlooking the nearby river. It had been raining, but the few remaining clouds and the filtered light of the setting sun served to add depth to the beautiful panorama before us. Manicured lawns sloped down to the water's edge. Ferries passed by at regular intervals, while smaller boats bobbed around in the bay below. Inside the restaurant, the sandstone walls glowed as candles were lit. What a privilege to enjoy this moment, I thought, given in love by our daughter and her family.

The manager kindly answered our various questions and we made our selections. Then, as we waited for our meal, I sat back and decided to forget about what it had cost our daughter and her husband and simply appreciate it all. Even now, as I remember the main course that soon arrived, my mouth waters. It turned out to be succulent and flavoursome, cooked to perfection and served with elegance – a treat for the eyes and the taste

buds. As for the dessert – well, anyone for a light, tempting, melt-in-your-mouth mango soufflé?

Yet at times that evening, I still found myself struggling with strange, doubt-filled thoughts. Did I deserve such a special meal? Was it okay for us even to be here in this beautiful, top-class restaurant? Were we merely interlopers in someone else's world, pretending we belonged? Perhaps they would throw us out at any moment. But then I remembered that, while we would not have to pay for our special dining experience, *someone* already had – and they truly wanted us to enjoy it.

Later, I realised this whole wonderful experience could be seen as a mini-parable of God's amazing grace in freely forgiving us and accepting us through faith in Jesus. What an enormous 'voucher' was extended to us that day on the cross, paid for by God's own Son! Yes, we are unworthy to receive it. Yet how sad if we were to ignore or misuse such a loving, gracious gift and resist walking into all the freedom and joy of living as God's child. Refusing to enjoy the gift of a beautiful meal is one thing, but refusing to accept the gift of God's grace is an enormous tragedy indeed.

May you and I receive God's amazing gift of new life with open, grateful hearts and continue to live each day in the joy of truly belonging to the family of God.

He came to that which was his own, but his own did not receive him. Yet to all who did receive him, to those who believed in his name, he gave the right to become children of God.

John 1:12

On God's Love and Grace

Heartfelt Words

The moment had come. For some time, I had planned to clean out a drawer stuffed with precious memorabilia – cards and notes received from family and friends over the years, old school reports, certificates for music and academic achievements, programmes from concerts and shows I had attended. I did not want to throw any of these precious items out but knew I should not put this rather daunting task off any longer.

First, I tackled all the cards. Many were beautiful, thank-you notes from groups where I had spoken or readers who had appreciated my books and taken the time to let me know. Others were special birthday or Mother's Day cards from our grandchildren, some handmade, with lovely messages inside written in wobbly letters. After reading them all again, I decided it was probably time to throw away most of the thank-you notes at least. But . . . surely I could keep those precious Mother's Day cards, couldn't I?

I dug deeper and found more home-made Mother's Day cards, this time from our own children, including one that said, 'You will like this present . . . and it only cost $1.49!' I found some funny notes as well, such as the following that made me smile all over again: 'Dear Mum and Dad, could you please make sure that in the morning my sister does *not*, I repeat, *not* wake me up and play the piano? Thank you. *Warning*: If she *does* do this offensive thing, you will probably *not live* to regret it – and that goes for her too! From your loving daughter.' Still another was in distinctly grovelling mode: 'Mummy darling dearest, if you are in a fantastic mood, PTO. If not, don't bother!' How could I throw such gems out?

On God's Love and Grace

I kept digging and soon found many more cards given or sent to me at key points in my life – cards when moving on from jobs; cards congratulating me on my graduation from theological college; cards on the death of my mother; cards on leaving our church; cards for no reason at all except to encourage me. So many words written just for me. So many words expressing so much love and heart-felt thanks for things I had said or done, some of which I now have no memory of ever saying or doing.

As I completed my mammoth task, I felt quite sad and nostalgic. I sat still for a while, trying to let all the love and affirmation that people had expressed truly sink in. Then in the quiet, I sensed God saying, 'Remember my own words I have said to you too, and take them to heart.' Soon, one after another, various precious snippets from Scripture began to come clearly to mind:

I will never leave you nor forsake you.

Joshua 1:5b

Do not let your hearts be troubled. You believe in God; believe also in me.

John 14:1

I will not leave you as orphans; I will come to you.

John 14:18

You did not choose me, but I chose you and appointed you so that you might go and bear fruit – fruit that will last.

John 15:16a

Heart-felt, encouraging words from family and friends are treasures indeed, but may we also treasure and take to heart God's loving, gracious words that are even more precious.

On God's Love and Grace

Is That Enough?

At one stage, our daughter worked for a well-known charitable organisation and would at times find herself taking phone calls from people wanting to make a financial donation. One of the most memorable conversations she had went something like this:

'Good morning! How can I help you?'

'I'd like to donate a thousand dollars to the foundation.'

'Did you say *one thousand dollars*?'

'Um . . . is that enough?'

Was this gentleman honestly thinking this might be too small a sum for them to accept? Our daughter suspected he had given more in previous years and felt bad he could no longer do the same – but what a strange question! Alternately, was he perhaps sincerely questioning his own level of generosity and thinking a thousand dollars was in fact a mere pittance, after all?

Sadly, the question he asked is all too familiar to me because, as a perennial people-pleaser, I have often asked it of myself. In all sorts of contexts, even when I have done my best, I can still wonder over and over, 'Was that enough? Was it what they wanted?' Whenever a visitor at our dinner table eats everything on their plate, I wonder if I gave them enough. Are they perhaps still hungry? Are they thinking what a mean hostess I am? If this happens at a family gathering, one of our children will usually roll their

eyes, jump in and say what they know I am about to say, simply to tease me: 'Did you have enough, dear? Would you like some more?'

People-pleasers want everyone to think well of them. They cannot bear to let anyone down or upset anyone because it is up to them to keep everyone happy. Yet how exhausting that can become – and how impossible to achieve anyway.

Sometimes, we can have the same attitude towards God too. When I was in my early teens, I thought that, if I went to church on any given Sunday, surely this would put me in God's good books for that week at least. Surely everything would go well because God would be so pleased with me. Thankfully, a few years later, I came to experience more of the amazing love and grace of God and to realise there is no point in my trying to impress God because I could never be good enough. Instead, Jesus, the perfect, sinless Son of God, has taken care of that for me on the cross and become all the 'enough' I need.

God showed his great love for us by sending Christ to die for us while we were still sinners.

Romans 5:8, NLT

God saved you by his grace when you believed. And you can't take credit for this; it is a gift from God. Salvation is not a reward for the good things we have done, so none of us can boast about it.

Ephesians 2:8–9, NLT

It is not about measuring up. It is not about making sure we have done enough to get into God's good books. Instead, it is about receiving the amazing grace we have been offered through Jesus Christ, then doing our best to honour him in the way we live each day. May each of us remember this when the pesky question, 'Is that enough?' next pops into our minds.

On God's Love and Grace

The Things We Do

I suspect all of us can think of times in our lives when we have had to do things way outside our comfort zones. Recently, I spoke somewhere on the topic of public speaking itself, and was quite shocked at the number of people present who said they hated the thought of ever doing such a scary thing. Perhaps these people may get by in life without ever having to speak in public, but probably all of us at some point have needed to ask someone for a reference, either written or verbal, in order to apply for a job. This can indeed be scary, can't it? Just this past week, a friend told me how, when she asked a teacher for a reference on leaving high school, this teacher said there was nothing positive she could think to say about her. Oh dear.

There can be many other occasions in life that may cause us to feel vulnerable and uncomfortable. Fronting up at job interviews, for example, can be challenging, as can even applying for them in the first place, depending on the information we are asked to submit about ourselves. Over the years, I have completed various manuscript submissions for potential publishers and initially found it rather daunting to have to promote myself in this way, explaining, as requested at times, why they should accept my manuscript over someone else's and what qualified me to be the best person to write such a book. In recent years too, I have often emailed various community groups to let them know I am available as a speaker, should they require one, and have had to overcome the fear that I may sound too pushy or egotistical in the process.

Then there are those times when, on completing a non-fiction book in particular, I have had to search for some people who may be willing enough to endorse my latest offering. These requests are indeed ones I mull

over many times before pressing the 'send' button on such an email. After all, it is a big ask to expect someone in a busy ministry role – or busy role of any description – to read one's manuscript, however well one knows them, then write something they are happy for all to read. Besides, what if they dislike or cannot agree with some things I have written? That could well be embarrassing all round.

I can still cringe now at such tasks, but there are several things these days that help me overcome my reluctance. First, I remind myself that what I have written is something I sensed God wanted me to write – and indeed has given me the ability to write. So I need to be faithful and obedient and see the project through to completion.

Second, in any situation involving potential embarrassment or rejection, I have learnt to take great comfort from the fact that God knows me through and through, accepts me fully, believes in me and loves me with a perfect love that no one can take away from me.

I have loved you with an everlasting love;
> **I have drawn you with unfailing kindness**.

Jeremiah 31:3b

I am God's child. I belong to God who will never reject me. That changes the whole picture for me – and I hope for you too.

On God's Love and Grace

Cornered

I enjoy board-games – well, many of them anyway. My sister and I grew up playing endless rounds of Snakes and Ladders, Ludo, Chinese Checkers, Draughts and Monopoly, not to mention Dominoes, Pick Up Sticks and a little quiz game called 'Tell Me'. There were card games too – children's ones at first such as Donkey, Old Maid, Comic Families and good old Snap and, later, Coon Can, Euchre and Five Hundred.

Nowadays, however, children's games somehow seem to have become trickier – for me at least. Our two younger grandchildren still enjoy their Snakes and Ladders, Monopoly, Dominoes and Donkey, but, well . . . what sort of person would think up such annoying, confusing games as one our 11-year-old grandson introduced me to recently, called 'Exploding Kittens'? Ugh!

Our grandson is excellent at explaining the rules of any game and did his best this time around, then patiently continued helping me. Yet it seemed that, whatever card I chose to throw out, something worse happened to me until eventually our grandson could block my every move. Then, of course, I ended up becoming the victim of that dreaded 'exploding kitten'.

At least this experience was marginally better than the time a few weeks ago when he tried to teach me how to play Chess. We gave him his Chess set some time back but, suddenly, he has taken to it in a big way, strategically plotting his moves well ahead. Meanwhile, I had to be told the names of the various pieces over and over and what they are allowed and not allowed to do. No wonder I ended up cornered in this game too, with nowhere to go.

On God's Love and Grace

At times, life can be like that too, can't it? For whatever reason, sometimes we find ourselves in a real-life, board-game situation where we can feel cornered, even powerless, with very few options available to us. Perhaps we end up stuck in some exhausting job, ongoing argument, draining relationship or debilitating health challenge where there seems to be no way out for us – and that can be very hard indeed.

I remember a time years ago when I was employed in a demanding teaching job, which left me feeling exhausted and trapped. I knew I had to keep going to help pay our mortgage at the time but, each Sunday, my heart sank as I thought of the week ahead. In the end, God graciously provided a way out of that job and into an editing role I loved. Yet it does not always happen like that, does it? Sometimes in life, there is no way of escape. Instead, we have to press on, doing our best to remain positive as we look to God for the strength and courage we need. Yet God is surely right there beside us and in us, comforting and encouraging us, even as we walk through those deep, dark valleys – and will be for ever.

Whatever your situation right now and however cornered you feel, I pray you will sense our strong Shepherd's hand on your shoulder today and know again his deep love and compassion for you.

Even when I walk through the darkest valley, I will not be afraid, for you are close beside me. Your rod and your staff protect and comfort me.
Psalm 23:4, NLT

On God's Love and Grace

Where Are You?

Life is full of new experiences. There is always some fresh challenge around the corner – and this was certainly the case on one occasion when our daughter bequeathed her two cats to us to mind while she travelled overseas. I began to learn so much as I observed those cats trying to come to terms with their new environment, not to mention the two rather weird people living there who were clearly novices at caring for cats.

It was soon obvious one cat was more adventurous than the other. After the initial shock had worn off, Tesla was prepared to emerge from hiding and start to explore. Soon she became daring enough to nuzzle our legs. Then she graduated to prowling around my desk, settling on my lap and nudging my hand whenever I had the audacity to stop stroking her so I could type. Coaxing her over to the nearby bed worked occasionally but only when she deigned it to be so. Eventually, she found an empty box and was in heaven for a while. But then that paper bin under my desk began to look interesting too. The result? Mess everywhere.

Meanwhile, on arrival, poor Lexxi bolted for a spot underneath our sideboard and stayed put. But when we looked for her there the next day, she was nowhere to be seen. Picture this then, if you can – two mature adults with worried looks, hunting high and low in every nook and cranny for said cat, moving beds, fridges and clothes driers, crawling on hands and knees under desks, peeking in boxes, behind curtains and even in cupboards that had been closed all along. You name it, we did it on and off for hours.

On God's Love and Grace

Eventually, after concluding she must have somehow escaped outside, we found her curled up on a tiny ledge behind an old desk in my husband's study where we were sure no cat would ever fit. We let her be, taking food and water to her. Then, finally, she braved it enough to gravitate during the night to a spot behind the settee in our lounge room where she remained silent and still – at least while we were around.

What did I learn from this experience? Apart from some practical tips on caring for cats, it inspired me to reflect on how often we human beings may try to hide from God. At times, we seem to revert so easily to the behaviour exhibited by Adam and Eve in the garden of Eden when they heard the Lord looking for them and hid in fear. Yet God knows where we are at every moment – just as I knew timid Lexxi's new hiding-place was behind the settee because the curtains pulled to one side there were a dead giveaway. God longs for us to emerge from our hiding-place, experience so much more of the warm, loving relationship and true freedom available to us and trust our faithful Owner to care for us well.

So where are you right now? Could you perhaps be hiding too? Is there more of God's amazing love and grace out there for you to explore? I certainly know there is for me.

Taste and see that the Lord is good; blessed is the one who takes refuge in him.
Psalm 34:8

On God's Love and Grace

Those Important Little Words

'Nanna, why do you say "love" all the time to me?' our 6-year-old granddaughter asked me one day.

'Pardon?' I responded, wondering what she could mean.

'Why do you call me "love" all the time?'

Before I had a chance to say anything, she answered her own question. 'I guess it's because you love me,' she said in a satisfied tone.

'Yes, I do,' I told her, 'and I want to let you know that.'

She went on with her day then, quite happy with herself and the world in general. But this little interlude set me thinking. Yes, I love her – and her brother, whom I also often called 'love' that day as we minded them. But I am aware it has been a habit of mine for years to call lots of people 'love'. Nowadays, the word slips out without my even realising it – and, in those all-too-often 'senior moments' when I forget someone's name, it can indeed be a handy and hopefully not too inappropriate substitute.

I also recall the loving way my special 'soul friend', Joy, used to greet me each time I arrived at her door to meet with her. 'Oh, hello, dear friend. *So* lovely to see you again. Come in!' she would say, smiling. On the odd occasions when she would email me, she would often begin with 'Dear friend' too, or perhaps 'My very dear Jo-Anne' instead. Somehow, these loving ways she addressed me touched and encouraged me even before I began reading anything else she had written. Through these little greetings alone, I knew Joy loved me and valued our friendship. I felt treasured

On God's Love and Grace

and significant – and I also sensed that, whatever other words her email contained, they would have been chosen with much thought and care and with a heart to bless me.

The way we speak to one another can be so important, can't it? But I wonder if you have thought about the words God loves to use when speaking to you and me, and have truly taken them in. If others can touch our hearts and encourage us via a few loving words, how much more can God do the same for each one of us?

One evening many years ago when I was in quite an exhausted state, I believe God gave me a picture of Jesus, holding me in his arms as a baby and looking down at me with the most amazing love and delight shining from his face. All he kept saying, over and over, was, 'Wow – Jo-Anne! Wow – Jo-Anne!' Through that simple yet utterly profound experience, I knew deep in my heart that Jesus saw me as his precious creation, that he was delighted with me, that he valued me and that he would always love and care for me. I can hear his voice even now, saying those same words over and over, and they still have the power to speak love and grace into my spirit.

May you too, even today, hear the same gentle voice speaking clearly to you, calling you by name, letting you know you are indeed God's much-loved child, highly valued and treasured.

See how very much our Father loves us, for he calls us his children, and that is what we are!

1 John 3:1, NLT

On God's Love and Grace

So Valued

It can be uplifting, can't it, when others sincerely value us and what we offer? It can make us stand taller and straighter, feel stronger and more whole and even help us see the world around us in a much more positive light.

Recently, our son bought a selection of books I have written as gifts for the teachers in his school staffroom. I was surprised at his request but happy to oblige. Yet it was more than that, I realised, as I helped him choose which book might best suit each teacher. I felt touched and honoured that he valued me not only as a mum but also as a writer – that he thought enough of my books to give them as gifts to his colleagues and wanted them to see my name on the front of each book, which of course is also his surname.

Perhaps this balances out a little our 12-year-old grandson's opinion of me, whom he often delights to tease by calling me 'just an old lady'! I have pointed out to him more than once that, while I may not know much at all about the various computer games and programmes he is so skilled at, I have other strengths. I also have two university degrees, as well as a couple of diplomas, but they, of course, mean little to him at this stage – and neither do the ten books and hundreds of blogs I have written. Yet underneath it all, I know he loves and values me, if the warm hugs he gives me at times are anything to go by. And I hope and pray he will continue to value me, the older he becomes.

Some may argue that Christians should show more humility than this and that we are not to look to others to boost our self-esteem or feed our vanity. Recently, I heard of an instance where someone was asked to name something they feel they do well. They refused to respond because they

On God's Love and Grace

seemed to think that would be showing too much pride in themselves and their achievements. Yet surely it is wise to know what we do well so we can live and serve in a way that brings joy to ourselves and others, as well as glory to God? Surely we can do this without becoming too puffed up with pride as we remember who gave us the gifts we have?

Surely too, we can seek to pass on to others something at least of the value our heavenly Father places on each one of us. Psalm 139 states that God knows us intimately and is always there, watching over us. And Jesus' words to his disciples on one occasion are certainly reassuring to us too:

Are not two sparrows sold for a penny? Yet not one of them will fall to the ground outside your Father's care. And even the very hairs of your head are all numbered. So don't be afraid; you are worth more than many sparrows.
Matthew 10:29–31

Above all, however, we see just how much more God values us than those sparrows when we remember how Jesus came to earth for our sakes and paid the ultimate price to save us.

We are indeed loved and valued. May we in turn love and value others too.

On God's Love and Grace

Breaking Through the Barrier

Some years ago, I had the privilege of driving a good friend to the airport. She was returning to work that she loved in Turkey, knowing full well that, in all likelihood, she would not see her family and friends for at least two years. It was therefore a bittersweet moment when the time came for us to say goodbye. Our friend's heart was in Turkey but also here with family and friends.

As soon as she disappeared into the customs area, our slightly teary group began to disperse. However, some of us decided to move to a spot beside a glass wall where passengers can be seen as they make their way to the departure gates. Soon we saw our friend, smiling at us and waving, then turning for one final backward glance before disappearing from view. We tried to communicate with her in various ways, blowing kisses and gesticulating wildly. Meanwhile, I noticed other passengers coming right up to the glass and placing their hands on it, in an effort to reach out to those friends and family on our side one more time. We were glad we had stayed for this final farewell, but it was not the same. That glass barrier stopped us from being heard, from hugging our friend and from communicating as freely as we had earlier.

As I thought about this experience, I realised that sometimes this is how it is between God and me. God is always there, wanting to communicate and be in close relationship with me. But sometimes barriers spring up between us – barriers that I either deliberately put in place or inadvertently allow to grow bigger and bigger over time. I want to talk things over with God heart to heart, and truly want God to speak to me 'face to face, as one speaks to a friend', as Moses experienced (Exodus 33:11). I want God to be

On Connecting with God

intimately involved in all areas of my life. Yet for some unknown reason, I distance myself at times behind one barrier or another. I might decide not to let go of something I know is spoiling our communication – perhaps anger or unforgiveness or lack of trust. Or I might allow myself to become too focused on my writing or too concerned about preparing for speaking engagements so that God's loving voice becomes more and more indistinct and the wonderful light of God's presence dims. I know God is there as surely as my friend was there smiling at us from behind that glass wall – but I cannot hear what is being said or feel that restoring, encouraging, comforting touch I need.

I do not want to live like that. I do not want to be alienated from the One who breathes life, creativity, courage and strength into my spirit. Through his death, Jesus has broken down the barrier separating us from God – so why do we insist on re-erecting it in our lives? Instead, may we learn to value our close connection with God so much more, and truly cherish God's loving, intimate presence with us each day.

Come close to God, and God will come close to you. Wash your hands, you sinners; purify your hearts, for your loyalty is divided between God and the world.

James 4:8, NLT

On Connecting with God

Finding Those 'Thin Places'

I wonder if you can think of a time or place when you almost held your breath because God seemed so close to you, perhaps even almost tangible. Back in the seventh century or thereabouts, the Celtic Christians in Britain and Ireland described this as being a 'thin place' – a setting or occasion when the separation between heaven and earth or God and human beings seemed almost to disappear and the two blended together in perfect harmony.

Does your heart long for such places and experiences? I know mine does. They can happen in all sorts of ways, I have discovered – even when we least expect them.

One day, I decided to sit down at our piano and play some of my old, classical pieces of music. I am out of practice but tried to do as much justice as I could to the beautiful melodies of Brahms, Beethoven, Mozart and others. Memories came flooding back as I did but, alongside them, I felt the distinct presence of God. It was as if God's heart was reaching out to me through those notes and speaking straight into my spirit, inspiring me through the creative works of others as I cooperated by bringing my own creative ability to the moment.

Perhaps you have experienced such times of closeness with God as you have gazed in awe at a beautiful coastline scene or mountain vista or observed God's creativity in the intricate design of a tiny flower. Perhaps this has happened for you during a time of worship or prayer as you have reflected alone or gathered with other believers. Perhaps you have even sensed God close by while you were in the middle of the hustle and bustle of a busy street

or a noisy crowd – and perhaps those of you who are authors will also be familiar with God's close, encouraging presence as you attempt to write words that will minister to others. In all these situations, we need to have our ears attuned to that still, small voice of the Spirit and our eyes focused not only on what we see before us but, beyond that, on our ever-present God.

It seems such a shame that we so often miss out on these wonderful, life-giving encounters with the reality of God that go far beyond anything this world can offer. Of course, we are called to make a difference for God's kingdom right here and now, but that is not all there is. Because God's Spirit lives in those of us who believe, we will never be fully at home here on earth. Along with those great men and women of faith listed in Hebrews 11, we will always be 'foreigners and strangers on earth' (verse 13). So we need to find those thin places for our own wellbeing and spiritual survival – and, whenever we take time to look, God will be there, ever willing to meet with us.

You will seek me and find me when you seek me with all your heart. I will be found by you,' declares the LORD, 'and will bring you back from captivity.'
Jeremiah 29:13–14a

As you go about your life in the coming days, seeking God with all your heart, may you experience God in your own thin places and be deeply nourished and refreshed.

On Connecting with God

Spiritual Snakes and Ladders

Have you ever played Snakes and Ladders with a preschooler? Perhaps you too have had the joy of explaining that, if you land at the bottom of a ladder, you can climb right up it. On the other hand, you might also remember the deflated look you received when you passed on the bad news that landing on a snake's head means you have to slide down that slimy snake and thus lose so much hard-won ground.

Snakes and Ladders can definitely be a game of fluctuating fortunes so, when our grandchildren first learned it, I was quite happy to help them along and let them win. Besides, I soon discovered the game had its difficult moments numeracy-wise for one granddaughter, which made it a challenge for her at her age to work out which way she was supposed to head. Remembering, for example, that fifty is the next number after forty-nine can be tricky, after all.

Even at such a tender age, however, she soon became quite resourceful and occasionally employed some original but rather dubious tactics in order to win. One was to throw the die behind her back or somewhere far away. Then, when she picked it up, it would miraculously turn out to be a six! But another sounded much more spiritual and involved fervently praying aloud to God.

'Please, God, I really, *really* need a six! Pleeeaaase *listen* to me,' she would entreat in a plaintive, agonised voice, with tightly screwed-up face and hands cupped around the die. When she did manage to throw a six after praying, she would let out a sigh of relief and exclaim in a delighted voice, 'Oh, thank you, God – you *did* listen to me.'

On Connecting with God

At that point, I thought I should put her theology straight so I tried to explain that, whether she ended up throwing a six or not, God is still listening. I also explained that God does not always give us what we think we want or need. Yet I did not get much further than that for two reasons. First, my words seemed to be going straight over her head. Second, I found she had lost interest since she had already won the game.

While our granddaughter might not have understood me, I came away from this experience with the humbling impression that God was trying to make *me* understand something too. At times, I am sure I treat God like a Snakes and Ladders God, by crying out for help when things are not going well or disaster threatens and giving thanks only when I am rescued. Yet in my heart, I want to live more often in a place of rest and peace, knowing that, whatever happens, God is and always will be the same loving, powerful, awesome God. I want to live much more often as Paul urges us to live:

Do not be anxious about anything, but in every situation, by prayer and petition, with thanksgiving, present your requests to God. And the peace of God, which transcends all understanding, will guard your hearts and your minds in Christ Jesus.

Philippians 4:6–7

I hope and pray our grandchildren will also want this for themselves in the years ahead – and I hope and pray you too can experience God's deep peace, whatever is happening around you.

On Connecting with God

Big, Bold Prayers

We have to hand it to King David. So often in the psalms, he spurns any softly, softly approach when it comes to asking God for help. That is indeed different from many of the prayers I have prayed over the years in both public and private – and, at the risk of sounding quite judgemental, also very different from some I have heard others pray. At times, I know my prayers can become insipid and sadly lacking in any real faith. Of course, we want to honour God as we pray and not presume anything, but sometimes it feels as if we have perhaps forgotten what a powerful, able God we indeed have.

I have discovered, however, that God is truly gracious and does hear and answer our prayers, despite any shortcomings or slightly weird theology they may contain. God sees our hearts and knows what we need before we even ask (Matthew 6:8). As a result, God is never confused by the words we use when we pray, as King David understood well.

You have searched me, Lord,
and you know me.
You know when I sit and when I rise;
you perceive my thoughts from afar.
You discern my going out and my lying down;
you are familiar with all my ways.
Before a word is on my tongue
you, Lord, know it completely.

Psalm 139:1–4

Perhaps that is why David often seemed to feel free to cry out to God from his heart in such a bold, honest way, just as he does in the following prayer:

Contend, Lord, with those who contend with me;
fight against those who fight against me.

On Connecting with God

Take up shield and armour;
    arise and come to my aid.
Brandish spear and javelin
    against those who pursue me.

Psalm 35:1-3a

As I read these words, I found myself cheering David on and thinking how this prayer could apply to the challenges in my own life. Then I reached the end of verse 3 and stopped dead:

Say to me,
    'I am your salvation.'

Psalm 35:3b

Was David actually instructing God how to respond? It seemed to me he was saying to God: 'I *think* you said you'd save me. I was convinced of that – but now I'm not so sure. I want to know that deep down inside me, so please tell me it's true.' *The Message* version puts it this way: 'Reassure me: let me hear you say, "I'll save you."'

Yet there seems to be more to it too, given David's bold approach in the rest of the psalm. It is as if David goes on to call God to account – as if he is saying something like: 'God, this is what you told me you'd do for me, but it doesn't look like that's happening. So, if you tell me you're my salvation, you'd better make good on your promise because, if you don't, then you won't have lived up to your name.'

What a challenge David is to me in the honest way he talks with God. Yet God does not seem to take offence. In fact, we are told God viewed David as 'a man after his own heart' (1 Samuel 13:14; Acts 13:22).

May this be true of us too as we learn to pray bigger, bolder prayers just as David did.

On Connecting with God

Feeling the Flow

Years ago, I discovered something intriguing. One evening, I was in the middle of preparing a talk and had become a little stuck as I tried to organise my thoughts. So I decided to take a break and have a shower. To my surprise, as I stood there, letting the warm water flow over me and mulling things over, what I wanted to say simply fell into place. Somehow, it was as if the water was cleansing not only the outside of me but the inside too, washing away my muddy thoughts and bringing so much more clarity in the process.

Some might say it was the relaxing effect of the water flowing over me that cleared my mind – and I am sure that was part of it. But I suspect there was more to it too. It seemed to me that, as that physical water flowed over me, so did the living water of God's Spirit, inspiring and enabling me to express myself so much better. While I did not swallow any physical water, I could sense spiritual water filling me up on the inside, deep in my being, so that the right words began forming and bubbling away there, ready to flow out onto the page and eventually to my audience.

More recently, I experienced something similar for a period, only not in the shower this time. Late in the afternoon when no one else was around, I made my way up to the heated pool and spa only a short distance from our unit. I was quite out of practice as a swimmer so, each week, I would challenge myself to improve on my previous efforts and manage a few more lengths of the pool without stopping. Gradually, I began to enjoy the sensation of the water flowing under and around my body again, especially when I did not have to wonder whether I would be able to make it to the other end or not. Instead, I would let my mind mull over whatever story

or blog I was writing or whatever input I was preparing, and talk it all over with God as I swam.

However, it was afterwards while relaxing in the spa that I experienced the lovely, cleansing flow of both physical and spiritual water the strongest. As those super-warm bubbles surged around me and the water jets massaged my body, it was as if a curtain lifted from my mind, giving me much clearer direction for my writing projects. Then, once again, I sensed deep peace and joy filling me up inside – a gift, I believe, from the Lord, who still delights to provide living water for us today, just as was offered to the Samaritan woman at the well all those centuries ago (John 4).

How much I need that beautiful, life-giving water to fill me so it can overflow to others as I write and speak. How much we *all* need it, so we can each in our own way bring light and life to our hurting world.

On the last and greatest day of the festival, Jesus stood and said in a loud voice, 'Let anyone who is thirsty come to me and drink. Whoever believes in me, as Scripture has said, rivers of living water will flow from within them.'

John 7:37–8

On Connecting with God

Hidden Gems

A few years ago, our church celebrated the fifth anniversary of its renovated and revamped premises. To fill everyone in on the journey taken to get the building to its present state, photos taken at different stages of the remodelling were shown during our services. All up, it was a wonderful testimony to what can be achieved when a community trusts God and works together to bring a shared vision to reality.

Of all those inspiring images I saw that day, one in particular stayed with me. It was a photo of what looked like graffiti scribbled on the floor of the main auditorium. Apparently, the night before the carpet was to be laid there, some church members decided they would like to write prayers all over the floor – prayers that God would always be honoured in this space, that all who enter would sense the presence of God's Spirit and feel welcome and accepted, and that lives would be changed as a result. What a surreal feeling to realise our feet were resting not only on carpet but, more importantly, on all those prayers written and prayed on our behalf – hidden gems indeed.

I remembered then a similar, smaller project I was involved in years ago at another church. At that time, it was customary to hang handmade banners on our church walls to remind us of certain truths or words of Scripture. I had seen a banner at a conference somewhere that featured a vine covered in fruit and sensed we needed one like it in our own church. So some of us had set about creating one featuring a large, twirling grapevine, complete with several bunches of big, purple grapes, along with the words: 'Chosen to bear fruit'. Then, as we began attaching the grapes to the banner, we decided to write the names of the main streets in our area underneath

On Connecting with God

them. We felt this was a way of praying for all those living nearby, that God would transform their lives and that they would not only become the fruit of our labours but would, in turn, bear fruit for the kingdom themselves.

We prayed and we sewed, then prayed and sewed some more. For a long time, that banner hung on our church wall, reminding us why we were there and what God could bring about as we prayed. Ministry was often difficult in that area but, gradually, people did come to know God better and see God work in their lives.

Time passed and my husband and I moved on – and that banner eventually disappeared too. But I believe God heard the prayers we prayed, as well as those written beneath the carpet in our current church. Our role is to pray and ask – and God is not deaf to our pleas. The fruit will come in our own lives and in the lives of others as we continue to trust and faithfully share God's love. How blessed we are that we can pray to our gracious, loving God about everything and in all sorts of ways, including via those special gems hidden under carpet or cloth.

This, then, is how you should pray:
'Our Father in heaven,
hallowed be your name,
your kingdom come,
your will be done,
**   on earth as it is in heaven.'**

Matthew 6:9–10

On Connecting with God

Listening to the Shepherd's Voice

Many years ago, our daughter, who was only a small child at the time, was asked what she wanted to be when she grew up. Her answer was a doctor or – wait for it – a shepherd! She had heard Bible stories about shepherds and must have decided they were a kind-hearted lot who cared for others, both animals and humans. The interesting thing is that, while she did not take up either occupation, she nevertheless clearly demonstrates these traits in her life and is still a doctor or shepherd at heart. Several times, she travelled to Romania with a volunteer organisation to help disabled children there and now works in the area of disability care.

I think of her whenever I read Psalm 23. This psalm is so well-known that we are tempted to gloss over its richness and read it only at funerals. Yet it contains such encouragement for us in our daily lives and deep comfort too whenever we find ourselves in difficult situations.

The psalm begins with a wonderful, strong assertion that should not be overlooked: 'The Lord is my shepherd.' What a huge statement! David, its author, is declaring that Yahweh, the Most High God, the 'I AM' – the one whose name the ancient Hebrews regarded as being too holy and too awesome even to be spoken aloud – is prepared to take on the lowly role of a shepherd and, furthermore, to lead and guide us personally throughout our lives. That still blows my mind and immediately takes me back to my teenage years when I realised for the first time that the mighty God of the whole universe knew me and cared about me enough to send Jesus to die for me.

On Connecting with God

As the psalm continues to unfold, we discover many other wonderful statements about the Lord:

> He makes me lie down in green pastures,
>   he leads me beside quiet waters,
>   he refreshes my soul.
> He guides me along the right paths
>   for his name's sake.
> Even though I walk
>   through the darkest valley,
> I will fear no evil,
>   for you are with me;
> your rod and your staff,
>   they comfort me.

Psalm 23:2–4

The key focus in all this is the close, comforting presence of the Shepherd before and beside me, strengthening me, showing me the way forward, defending me, healing me. My task then is to ensure I keep my eyes on him, listening for his voice, trusting him when he takes me in a particular direction. These verses remind me too of Jesus' own words when he said: 'My sheep listen to my voice; I know them, and they follow me' (John 10:27).

What a privilege to have Jesus, the Good Shepherd who laid down his life for his sheep, intimately involved in my life journey, with all its twists and turns. Moreover, Jesus has told us this relationship will never end, that no one can snatch us out of his hand (John 10:28). The final words of Psalm 23 remind us of this too:

> Surely your goodness and love will follow me
>   all the days of my life,
> and I will dwell in the house of the LORD
>   for ever.

Psalm 23:6

May we always listen well to the voice of our loving Shepherd and allow him to lead us throughout our lives.

On Connecting with God

Letting Our Souls Live

Although there are only two of us in our household now, I seem to spend an inordinate amount of time each week deciding what our main meals will be, shopping for all the necessary ingredients and finally cooking. I also try to have a selection of things in the fridge and pantry to choose from for our lunches, including some cake for my sweet-toothed husband or any visitors who might drop in. All this takes planning and effort, but I do it because, after all, we need to eat – although perhaps not quite as much or as often as we do!

Lately, however, it has dawned on me that, in focusing on all this physical nourishment, I may well be short-changing myself in other areas. Like everyone else, I need emotional nourishment – the love of family and friends, the fulfilment gained through writing, the enjoyment of reading, listening to music, marvelling at the beauty of nature or watching an uplifting TV show. I know the danger of missing out on such things and I know I cannot give out to others in any meaningful way if my own emotional tank is empty. Yet when there is too much else to do, I can easily ignore such vital nourishment.

But what about the deepest part of us that we call our soul? It too needs to be nourished, perhaps even more so than our physical bodies and our emotions. If our souls are dead, if that light has gone out inside us, if that firm connection with God is lost, then life can indeed become rather dull and meaningless. We are not at peace with God or within ourselves – and that is certainly not the most pleasant way to live.

On Connecting with God

Recently, I read the following beautiful invitation found in Isaiah 55:

Come, all you who are thirsty,
come to the waters;
and you who have no money,
come, buy and eat!
Come, buy wine and milk
without money and without cost.
Why spend money on what is not bread,
and your labour on what does not satisfy?
Listen, listen to me, and eat what is good,
and you will delight in the richest of fare.
Give ear and come to me;
listen, that you may live.

Isaiah 55:1–3a

Yes, I decided, I need to take time to come and enjoy that rich fare my soul longs for. So one morning, I headed to a nearby spot with a beautiful lake surrounded by bushland. I used to go there regularly to reflect, write, enjoy the beauty of nature and be with God but, somehow in the busyness of life, this had slipped from my agenda. How wonderful it was that morning to sit there again, with the sun warming me all over as I contemplated the lake before me. The breeze ruffled the surface of the water so that it sparkled in the sun, while nearby, a family of ducks swam serenely past. I savoured it all, sensing God's presence everywhere around me. Soon I could feel a wonderful peace deep inside, bringing much-needed refreshment and breathing life into my soul once again.

May your soul be nourished and renewed too as you take time to draw close to God, listen well and delight in that richest of fare only our wonderful God can provide.

On Connecting with God

Alert and Still

I glance up from my desk and notice a rather impressive visitor sitting on the balcony railing outside my study window – a kookaburra, looking as if it owns everything within view. I move to take its photo through the glass and it turns its head as if to say, 'I know you're there but I also know I'm safe from you out here.' Some smaller, noisy birds do not like that larger, alert presence nearby and try to frighten the kookaburra away by squawking loudly and bombarding it. Yet it remains immovable, except for a slight shuffle along the railing and a few sharp turns of its head. Its eyes are on a nearby prize – perhaps something for dinner that those other birds also want?

As I watch, I marvel at how still that kookaburra stays. No doubt it is extremely alert to what is happening around it – and that soon becomes obvious when it suddenly flies down to ground level, then plucks a poor, unsuspecting worm from the soil. In a few moments, that worm is no more. All the quiet watchfulness the kookaburra displayed has finally paid off – it has found its dinner.

At that point, I begin to suspect God is teaching me an important lesson through this little scenario. I might be physically still as I gaze at the kookaburra but I am not mentally still. Even while I watch, my mind is darting this way and that as I wonder whether my writing makes sense or will amount to anything. Deep inside, I am not still either. Instead, I feel somewhat stressed – I am worried about someone we hold dear who is facing many difficulties and also about an upcoming speaking engagement, not to mention my writing project. I am aware God knows about all these issues, yet I struggle to stay in a place of stillness and peace with God, of complete trust that God has it all under control.

On Connecting with God

I move my hands away from my keyboard and lay them in my lap. I breathe deeply, letting my body relax. I picture God's loving arms holding me close and sink back into them, sensing God's Spirit both in me and around me. I still my mind and my heart, knowing it is enough to be in this present moment with God. Then I remember some words read out at church only days ago:

God is our refuge and strength,
**   an ever-present help in trouble.**
Therefore we will not fear, though the earth give way
**   and the mountains fall into the heart of the sea . . .**
. . . Be still, and know that I am God;
**   I will be exalted among the nations,**
**   I will be exalted in the earth.**

Psalm 46:1–2,10

In the stillness, a gentle voice also reminds me that I am in a daily battle with an age-old enemy and need to remain vigilant and aware of his tactics:

Be alert and of sober mind. Your enemy the devil prowls around like a roaring lion looking for someone to devour.

1 Peter 5:8

May we all become much more alert and watchful, like that kookaburra outside my window. But may we also still our hearts and be at peace as we remember our loving, almighty God is always watching over us.

Locating Those Lights

I was aware it would be a long drive to my friend's book launch but I wanted to attend. Having launched a few books of my own, I knew what it felt like to put our creations out there in public, particularly for the first time. Besides, I had been involved in editing this particular book in its final stages and was also at the writers' conference where my friend received her publishing contract. I remembered that joyful moment well – and now I looked forward to sharing another equally joyful one with her.

I headed south from Sydney along the coast, a drive that normally takes around two hours. All went well until the rain came, followed by heavy fog, which blanketed the surrounding bushland and road ahead so that I could barely see the tail-lights of the car in front. Then I noticed a large sign flashing above the road that was almost illegible in the fog too. Eventually, however, I was able to make out what it said: *Use hazard lights in fog. Stay under 70kph.*

I slowed down but wondered if I could perhaps do without those hazard lights. Anyway . . . where *were* they? I knew where to locate them in my husband's new car, but where were they in my own ancient Ford that has done over 260,000 kilometres? After all, I had driven it only for around twenty-one years!

At that point, I noticed how most other cars nearby had their hazard lights on. I hunted around for a red triangle but still could not find it. Then, in a moment of inspiration, I peered behind the steering wheel and discovered a mysterious, red button there. I pressed it – and, to my relief, my hazard lights started flashing.

On Connecting with God

I reached the book launch safely and, by the time I drove home, the fog had largely lifted. But as I thought about my rather scary experience, I began to wonder if God had something to say to me through it all. How often have I felt as if a thick fog has settled around me so that I cannot seem to find God – especially when I am overbusy? How often have I not noticed the big warning sign across my path, reminding me to draw close to God again? Indeed, how often have I deliberately ignored it, thinking I can manage everything in my own strength?

Travelling through a fog, whether physical or spiritual, can be dangerous. We can feel helpless, directionless and confused. How desperately we need to be aware of hazard lights – and the Saviour's strong presence right beside us, protecting us and showing us the way forward. In a physical fog, one mistake could result in disaster. In a spiritual fog, we may find ourselves in an even more disastrous situation when we forget who God is and how God longs to walk with us each day, loving us, guiding us, watching over us.

However dense the fog in our lives might be right now, may we reach out to God for the guidance and help we need, keeping our eyes focused on the true Light that can illuminate even the darkest road ahead.

For this God is our God for ever and ever;
    he will be our guide even to the end.

Psalm 48:14

On Connecting with God

How Could This Be?

From time to time in my life, I meet people who make me sit up and take particular notice of them. Somehow, they seem to march to the beat of a different drum – and I want to find out what that drum is and how to keep in step with it.

Years ago, after moving across Sydney, we met a couple whose Christian commitment and experience of God seemed so much more real than mine was at that point. One day, I decided I could not wait any longer to find out more.

'What is it you've got that I haven't got?' I asked them point-blank.

At first, they looked at each other as if unsure how to answer me. In the end, all they said was, 'Just wait – just wait. God will show you when the time's right.'

I found this response frustrating, if not plain annoying at the time but, as it turned out, they were right. Not long after, God broke into my life in a fresh, wonderful way, overwhelming me with deep love and opening up a whole new journey of being led by the Spirit in my life and ministry.

I was reminded of this conversation again not long ago when farewelling a friend at the airport. The person at the check-in counter discovered a possible issue with my friend's visa so took it to her boss. When she returned, she told my friend it 'should all be okay', which did not sound reassuring to me at all. But my friend stayed calm and seemed to take everything in her stride.

On Honouring and Serving God

'You're so calm about it all,' the check-in person finally blurted out. 'It makes me want to say, "I'll have what she's having!"'

My friend and I looked at each other and laughed. You see, we had prayed for God's peace to surround her as she said goodbye to family and friends – and now this staff member was wondering why my friend was so calm. I mumbled something about how we had prayed about having peace but there was no time to explain further, with the queue lengthening behind us.

More recently, I met someone who decided to attend church again one Sunday after an absence of many years because of certain queries and doubts about the Christian faith. As the service ended, the pastors announced they would be delighted for anyone with questions about God and Jesus to come and chat with them afterwards.

'What church ever does anything like that?' this person thought, amazed – and promptly took them up on their offer.

But one of the best examples of amazement I have ever seen or heard can be found in John 7. Here, the people of Jerusalem are trying to work out who Jesus is and how he can do the things he does. Some want to seize him, but 'no one laid a hand on him' (John 7:44). Finally, the temple guards return to those in authority, who ask why they have not arrested Jesus. Then comes this incredible statement:

'No one ever spoke the way this man does,' the guards replied.

John 7:46

How can this be? Could Jesus truly be the Messiah, the Son of God? Should we sit up and take notice of him?

I think we should, don't you?

On Honouring and Serving God

When We Are Good and Ready

It takes an effort to remember when I was a busy, young mum – it *is* quite a while ago, after all. But one recent morning, in the few seconds it took me to read one sentence from a story Jesus told, I found myself reliving an event from those years that impacted my life in a deep, ongoing way.

In my mind, I saw myself holding our baby son again in the crèche during a Sunday morning service. As I stood rocking him, someone in the church began reading Matthew 18:21–35 aloud, the parable of the unmerciful servant. I was listening but was also distracted and concerned about our son who was quite unwell. Yet as soon as I heard the servant's response – "'Be patient with me," he begged, "and I will pay back everything"' (verse 26) – something happened inside me. Why did these words jump out at me? After all, they are nothing more than a simple cry for mercy. Yet God used them in an amazing way, completely out of their context in this story, to speak to me that morning. In an instant, God had my attention.

As the service continued, I heard nothing more – not even the input from the excellent visiting speaker about the real point of this story Jesus told. It was as if an electric current had run through me and I had been shocked into seeing my life much more clearly. You see, through those few words, I knew God was saying to me in a loving but firm, confronting way, 'This is how you have been treating me, Jo-Anne.'

I was a young mum with two small children at the time. I was busy with so many things – looking after my family, cooking, gardening, sewing, shopping, cleaning. I was also involved in at least two ministries at our church. My faith was real, but I knew I had lost the close, intimate

On Honouring and Serving God

relationship with God I once had. If I ever found any spare time during my day, I would rarely decide to spend it with God. Instead, I would choose to do all the other things I liked so much more – playing the piano, singing, reading, writing letters. After all, God would still be there when I was less busy and had nothing more interesting to do.

In essence, I had been saying to God, 'Just be patient – you can wait. When I'm good and ready, I'll spend more time with you.' What an insult! How dare I treat my loving, heavenly Father in this way?

I felt as if a knife had been plunged through me and remember thinking, 'So this is what that little phrase "cut to the heart" must mean.' I knew I could never repay the huge debt I owed God for sending Jesus and for saving me – I did not need to anyway. But surely I needed to give God first place in my life, along with all due honour and respect?

That morning, a whole new, more intimate journey with God began. Today, I am still reaping the benefits of God's grace in challenging my 'when I'm good and ready' attitude back then – and God's ongoing patience too.

May we love and serve God not only when we are good and ready but all the time.

On Honouring and Serving God

A Love Rekindled

I love candles and often like to have one burning on my desk as I write. This passion began years ago, although I cannot remember how or why. From time to time, I forget about how nice they are but, whenever someone who knows me well gives me another one, that passion is soon rekindled, along with my new candle.

I remember once mentioning this love of candles in a training group and receiving some incredulous looks, particularly from the younger men present. What is she *on* about, they were clearly wondering. Has she lost it altogether? What is so good about having a candle burning when working alone or when counselling or mentoring someone? Is this some superstitious rubbish?

Candles fulfil several functions for me. First, they serve as a tangible reminder to me of the presence of God as I sit at my desk, thinking and writing. I know God is with me anyway every moment of the day – but I can still often forget this. As I acknowledge God's presence in this way, I remember the following words that Jesus said:

I am the light of the world. Whoever follows me will never walk in darkness, but will have the light of life.

John 8:12b

How easily I can lose sight of that truth, allow the enemy to gain ground and let the darkness of discouragement take over.

Second, as I notice my candle burning, I am reminded of the light I endeavour to shine through my writing and speaking. Even though what I produce might be only one small, insignificant flame, it is still burning

On Honouring and Serving God

brightly and has the potential to shine God's light into someone's life. As Jesus reminded us, each one of us is called to do just that for others:

You are the light of the world. A town built on a hill cannot be hidden. Neither do people light a lamp and put it under a bowl. Instead they put it on its stand, and it gives light to everyone in the house.

Matthew 5:14–15

Third, there are aesthetic reasons behind my love of candles. I love their colours – beautiful purples, lilacs, blues and creams. I love the perfume of the scented ones – rose, vanilla, eucalypt. I love the ever-changing shape of the flame as it burns – darker at the centre, then lighter and brighter towards the tip. I love the sense of warmth and comfort candles bring to a room. During one trip to Europe, my friend and I stayed with a family in the Netherlands. When evening fell, our host would busy herself lighting the many candles dotted around their sitting-room. Then we would relax together in the gentle light, chatting and enjoying such warm fellowship, despite my being a stranger from the other side of the world. That warm, welcoming scene is etched forever in my memory.

Finally, as my candles burn, I love to remember the ones who gave them to me – my children, a good friend, a mentoree, my sister, a group where I once spoke. I pray that they too will know the presence of the Saviour, the Light of the World, with them at all times. I pray their light will continue to shine brightly wherever they are, today and always – and I pray that for you now too.

On Honouring and Serving God

Taking Jesus at His Word

It never ceases to amaze me how parts of Scripture we may have read many times before can still jump out and impact us all over again. They may challenge and rebuke – or at least make us rather uncomfortable – but what a privilege to receive these reminders over and over and know they come from the hand of our patient, wise, merciful Lord.

One day, I read and was touched once again by the account of Jesus' meeting with the Samaritan woman at the well. At the end of the same chapter, I then found the story of the royal official in Cana who asks Jesus to come and heal his son some distance away in Capernaum (John 4:46–53).

At first, Jesus seems reluctant: "'Unless you people see signs and wonders," Jesus told him, "you will never believe'" (verse 48).

But the official still insists he needs to come: "'Sir, come down before my child dies'" (verse 49).

Jesus then responds with a brief but huge statement of promise – and, lo and behold, the official takes him at his word and immediately leaves: "'Go,' Jesus replied, "your son will live." The man took Jesus at his word and departed' (verse 50).

Wow! Once again, I was amazed at the power and authority of Jesus' words – but the official's simple, unquestioning obedience made me sit up too. Perhaps he was among those who had witnessed Jesus in action in Jerusalem at the Passover Feast when Jesus cleared the traders and money-changers out of the temple and also performed miracles (John 2:13–25; 4:45).

On Honouring and Serving God

Yet, whether this is true or not, the official's firm belief in Jesus' promise that his son will be healed speaks volumes to me. Would I have been as ready to trust Jesus as he was? Would I have perhaps continued to beg him to come and actually lay hands on my son instead? Or would I have headed home, heart-in-mouth, filled half with hope and half with huge doubts?

The official does not get far, however, before his servants meet him with the news that his son is better. Then he discovers that this occurred at the exact time Jesus had declared his son would indeed live.

At that point, I received my second huge challenge of the day. All John writes in the next sentence are the following matter-of-fact words: 'So he and his whole household believed' (John 4:53b). Just like that, this official and his family believe in Jesus. Would that have been my response? Or would I have perhaps been tempted to rationalise things and not be too hasty about it all?

This whole experience certainly served to remind me with a jolt how powerful and trustworthy Jesus is and how I too need to take him at his word much more readily. If he says something will happen, it will happen. He does not lie or go back on his promise. If he tells us to do something, we had better do it – because Jesus, after all, is the holy Son of God. If Jesus says it, that settles it. And when he answers our requests today to heal us or rescue us or provide for us in some way, may we too respond with deep, unshakeable faith and give him our full allegiance all over again.

On Honouring and Serving God

The Best Boast of All

Have you ever noticed how some English words that have an unpleasant, negative meaning *sound* unpleasant as well? Take the words 'gloat', 'grudge', 'brag' and 'boast', for example, with their rather hard, guttural consonants. Or is it that their meaning colours how these words sound to us? Would someone unfamiliar with English still find them unpleasant?

One evening, I spoke to a community group about the lessons we learn throughout our lives and how, as we grow older, we hopefully become more of the person we were created to be. While talking about my own school years, I showed a photo of an old report card of mine and mentioned my determination to come first in every exam in primary school – which I eventually managed to do.

Immediately, I overheard a lady at a nearby table say in a rather nasty tone, 'Well, why don't you *brag* about it then?'

I had not meant to boast at all through sharing this part of my story. In fact, my aim was to point out how foolish I was to try to impress others with my academic achievements in order to become more popular. But that night, that little word 'brag' I overheard sounded particularly ugly and harsh to me – and I decided to respond.

'That's the very point I'm making,' I told the lady, who looked just a little embarrassed at that point. 'Why brag about such things? There's so much more to us than what we achieve or do well. It's foolish to depend on these things to impress others and gain friends.'

On Honouring and Serving God

Maybe I should have let the comment pass, but words such as 'brag' and 'boast' do not sit well with me. That may be why some words Paul wrote caught my eye soon after:

Brothers and sisters, think of what you were when you were called. Not many of you were wise by human standards; not many were influential; not many were of noble birth. But God chose the foolish things of the world to shame the wise; God chose the weak things of the world to shame the strong. God chose the lowly things of this world and the despised things – and the things that are not – to nullify the things that are, so that no one may boast before him.

1 Corinthians 1:26–9

Paul goes on to quote the prophet Jeremiah: 'Therefore, as it is written: "Let the one who boasts boast in the Lord"' (verse 31). When I read these words, I decided to turn to Jeremiah and check out the passage they come from for myself. There I found the following equally challenging words:

This is what the LORD says:
'Let not the wise boast of their wisdom
**   or the strong boast of their strength**
**   or the rich boast of their riches,**
but let the one who boasts boast about this:
**   that they have the understanding to know me,**
that I am the LORD, who exercises kindness,
**   justice and righteousness on earth,**
**   for in these I delight,'**
**   declares the LORD.**

Jeremiah 9:23–4

What a wonderful Lord we are privileged to know. Who else could ever treat us with such perfect justice and righteousness or show us such kindness? Only our Lord – and I am more than happy to be accused of boasting about him anytime.

On Honouring and Serving God

No Room

I wonder if you have ever concocted some excellent plan, only to have someone else come along with extra advice and mess everything up for you. Perhaps they might ask a simple question or suggest a better way forward, but we do not want to hear it because we have already invested so much time and energy into our plan. Or perhaps we feel we have finally come to understand some theological issue and know what we believe. Then someone comes up with a radically different idea that makes our whole concept – perhaps even our whole world – seem a little wobbly and threaten to come crashing down around us. In such instances, however well-intentioned the person might be, we may well feel like shouting at them, 'How *dare* you throw a spanner in the works like that!'

If you have ever felt this way, you might relate to the Jews in Jesus' time who, according to John 8, had apparently believed in him to some extent at that point. But then Jesus started talking about things like knowing the truth and being set free. What was *this* all about? Surely they were Abraham's descendants? Why would *they* need to be set from anything? They were fine, thank you very much. Moreover, this was very dangerous teaching. Much better to get rid of this Jesus if he was going to keep talking rubbish about things like pleasing his Father and being 'from above'.

Nevertheless, perhaps we should give them the benefit of the doubt. Maybe they had not heard about the amazing things Jesus had been doing, like changing water into wine, healing people, feeding more than five thousand with a few fish and loaves, not to mention walking on water. Yet whether they had or not, they decided there was no place for this crazy, insulting person in their world and that he was better out of the picture.

On Honouring and Serving God

But Jesus saw right through them. He knew they wanted to get rid of him – and he did not beat about the bush. In John 8:37 we read: 'I know you are Abraham's descendants. Yet you are looking for a way to kill me, because you have no room for my word' (John 8:37).

No room to hear what the Son of God had to say? What a sad, sad statement. These Jews seemed to be too full of pride in their heritage and too concerned about their own wellbeing to have any space in their hearts and lives to take Jesus' words on board at all. They felt they knew God in a special way – yet Jesus bluntly went on to tell them: 'The reason you do not hear is that you do not belong to God' (John 8:47b).

But what about us today? In fact, what about *me*? How often in my busy life do I simply have no room for God's word? Yes, I might read it when I feel like it or have time, but how often does it truly enter my heart? Worse still, just like these Jews, how often do I decide I do not like something God has said and refuse to make space in my life to put any necessary changes in place?

'You have no room for my word.'

May we truly hear Jesus' challenge and take it to heart today.

You Never Know

I wonder if you have ever run into someone you know in a most unexpected place. When I was a teacher, I well remember encountering one of my less well-behaved students in the middle of the supermarket. 'Mum, there's my teacher!' the girl blurted out, shocked. I suspect she wanted to see me about as much as I wanted to see her that day.

On another occasion, I ran into a pastor friend in a Christian bookstore. While we chatted, several others she knew came by. At first, I wondered if this might disconcert her a little but, instead, she seemed to enjoy the moment. 'It's like I've died and gone to heaven!' she exclaimed, beaming at everyone.

Recently, I headed to a medical facility for a shoulder injection. I was not expecting to see anyone I knew there – or anyone who knew me. All I was thinking was whether my scheduled injection would help alleviate my shoulder pain. Eventually, a young woman called my name and ushered me into a small room. We chatted as she prepared the injection for the doctor to give. A few moments later, it was all over, and the doctor left. Then, out of the blue, the young woman said to me, 'You must be the author, are you?'

I was stunned. 'Um . . . yes, but how did you know?' I eventually managed to ask.

'I've read some of your books,' she told me. 'I borrowed them from my mother.'

On Honouring and Serving God

So that was it – mystery solved. As a result, she had recognised my name on the patient list. But I was still curious.

'What would your mother's name be? Perhaps I know her too.'

Sure enough, I had indeed met her on several occasions.

'This shows we need to behave wherever we go, doesn't it?' I joked as I left. 'You never know who you'll meet.'

Yet even as I laughed along with this young woman, I was also trying to remember what comments I had made to her earlier in my visit. At the time, I had been so focused on myself that I had not put much thought at all into what I said. Had I been polite and considerate towards her? Had I listened well? Had I honoured God throughout our conversation?

It was too late now. The exchange was over.

I came away from that experience realising again that, wherever I go and whether I feel like it or not, I am representing God to others. I never know whom I will meet. I never know who will recognise my name, even though I am not a famous author – yet! I never know who will be listening or watching, but I am thankful God does. I am thankful too that God's Spirit is with me and in me, ready to give me the right words to share with others and the wisdom to act in a godly way. My task is to be alert, to listen and to be ready to say and do those things that truly honour God and bless others.

May I remember that well, because you never know . . .

He has committed to us the message of reconciliation. We are therefore Christ's ambassadors, as though God were making his appeal through us.
2 Corinthians 5:19b–20

On Honouring and Serving God

Keeping It Simple

One recent, crisp, sunny morning, my husband happened to stop and chat briefly with one of our elderly neighbours.

'It's a lovely day, isn't it?' our neighbour commented. 'I wouldn't be dead for quids.'

This man is in his mid-nineties so there is no doubt that, one day soon, he will indeed be dead whether he likes it or not. From the various conversations we have had with him, it is hard to tell if he has a personal faith in God. I hope he does and is ready to meet God because, however many quids he would be willing to wager to stay here and whether he truly believes in God or not, that day will surely come.

Recently, when we had to attend three funerals in one week, we were clearly reminded of the need to be ready for that day when our own lives will end. At one of these, that of another lovely neighbour, Ruth, the minister told everyone how he visited her not long before she passed away. During his time with her, Ruth apparently managed to share three very important words with him, despite being so weak and ill – 'I love Jesus.'

I cannot think of any better statement to make so close to the end of my life, can you? Three simple, little words, yet they say so much. When we experience the love Jesus has for us and truly believe as a result, then our spirits come alive and we are able to love him in return – and others – as we are called to do.

For this is how God loved the world: He gave his one and only Son, so that everyone who believes in him will not perish but have eternal life.

John 3:16, NLT

On Honouring and Serving God

We love each other because he loved us first.

1 John 4:19, NLT

Out of our love for Jesus, who showed us what perfect love is by dying for us, we are empowered to live in a way that honours him and be the faithful servants he has called us to be. Then, having loved and lived for him, we will be ready and waiting when he returns or when our time on earth is over. In fact, while we may not want to leave our loved ones behind here, just as Ruth may not have wanted to, we can look forward with anticipation to the day when we will meet Jesus face to face at last.

And as we live in God, our love grows more perfect. So we will not be afraid on the day of judgment, but we can face him with confidence because we live like Jesus here in this world.

1 John 4:17, NLT

What a privilege to know and love Jesus – and what a privilege to love and serve him and others each day as we live our lives here to the full. I understand what our elderly neighbour meant when he stated he would rather be alive than dead. Our life here has much to offer indeed. Yet I am so grateful I know death is not the end either – that, one day, I will go to be with Jesus, the one I love the most, who lives and reigns forever.

It truly is as simple as that – and as wonderful.

On Honouring and Serving God

Memories

It is amazing how our memories work and what interesting experiences can surface years after the event. Recently, while our children were at our place for a family birthday party, they began to regale my husband and me with stories of the things we used to let them do – or *not* do – when they were younger. We could not remember some of these at all – surely they had made them up? Yet they vowed each one was true.

Not long after that, I experienced my own set of even more precious memories while working my way through the book of Psalms again. There I was, happily reading along, when the following words transported me to another time and place in an instant:

Come, let us sing for joy to the Lord;
  let us shout aloud to the Rock of our salvation.
Let us come before him with thanksgiving
  and extol him with music and song.

Psalm 95:1–2

Even though these words are from a more modern Bible translation than what was available when I was young, in my mind, I heard them exactly as they had sounded in the Sunday-morning services I attended at our local church at that point. I could even hear the minister's voice as he led worship and the sound of the pipe organ that accompanied us. For a moment, I was back in that old church with its colourful, stained-glass windows and its gleaming brass cross and candlesticks on the altar, singing from the heart:

O come, let us sing unto the Lord: let us make a joyful noise to the rock of our salvation. Let us come before his presence with thanksgiving, and make a joyful noise unto him with psalms.

Psalm 95:1–2, KJV

On Honouring and Serving God

After emerging from this memory, I read on, only to stop again in the next psalm:

Ascribe to the LORD, all you families of nations,
**   ascribe to the LORD glory and strength.**
Ascribe to the LORD the glory due to his name.

Psalm 96:7–8a

This time, a much later memory from the nineties surfaced of a worship song written by one of our gifted musicians in the church we attended at the time. I remembered how this man would often look over his spectacles at me as I led worship, smiling and encouraging me, while he played the piano. What rich times we experienced as we praised God from our hearts via his original music.

I read on through the next few psalms and found so many snippets of sentences that reminded me of the old Scripture choruses we used to sing in the eighties with such joy and fervour. These simple choruses were a vital part of those years when I grew so much in God.

I am grateful for all these words of Scripture that have stayed in my mind as a result of singing them, ready to be unearthed as needed whenever God prompts. Music is powerful, in and of itself. But once combined with the power and authority of Scripture, such songs of praise can pierce our hearts and lift our spirits in an amazing way.

As we continue to sing God's word today then, together or alone and in whatever shape or form, may we do so with a truly thankful heart and with all our soul, mind and strength.

On Honouring and Serving God

Really?

Sometimes I hear myself saying the strangest things. Take, for example, those occasions when I have said to someone, perhaps after hearing about a challenge they recently faced, 'I hope everything went well for you in the end.' What I *really* mean is that I hope this person is okay *now*. Surely hoping some past event went well is a little pointless, apart from whatever empathy we may express in the process? The moment has passed, and all the hope we can muster will not change what happened back then.

Recently, while walking to my car, I saw a man nearby who was wearing the jersey of a particular football team. As he stood chatting to another man, I heard him say, 'Well, we believe in miracles.'

Initially, I thought to myself, 'Oh, that's wonderful – this man believes in miracles!'

But his next sentence made it clear what he *really* meant. 'With a little bit of luck, we might get there,' he declared.

I realised then that he must be talking about an upcoming football match and his doubt that his team would actually win. But the more I thought about his words, the more I began to wonder if he had expressed something of my own strange thinking at times. Yes, I believe God can do miracles. I have experienced them myself and seen them happen in the lives of others. I have read too about the amazing miracles Jesus performed and how God raised him from the dead. On top of that, I see miracles each day in the beauty and intricacy of nature around me. Yet to my shame, sometimes I suspect my prayers for someone to be healed or rescued from a difficult

situation can be more like a wish that luck might be on their side than a fervent, faith-filled plea to God on their behalf.

There is a big difference between the two, don't you think? When we pray, we are talking with the all-loving, all-knowing, all-powerful God of the universe. Our God is personal and alive. Our God is able to heal and renew, either supernaturally or through the care and expertise of others, including the medical profession. As well, our God is able to reach out in love and rescue us from our struggles and difficulties or give us the strength to walk through them, all the while comforting us deeply. On the other hand, relying on luck involves nothing more than believing in or appealing to impersonal, random forces, without knowing whether they will be on our side or not. All we can do in this case is hope for the best.

Years ago, there was a book around called *Your God is Too Small*, a title which still challenges me today. How often do I lose sight of who God really is? How often do I take my gaze off God and, instead, trust in some vague kind of luck? Have I indeed made God too small?

May we raise our sights, enlarge our vision, realise how great our God truly is and rest daily in God's loving grace, mercy and provision for each one of us.

Your ways, God, are holy.
   What god is as great as our God?
You are the God who performs miracles;
   you display your power among the peoples.

Psalm 77:13–14

On Honouring and Serving God

Reading the Directions

Some years ago, our daughter gave me a small, silver and gold tin for Christmas. Judging from the wonderful, gardenia-like perfume I could smell even before I opened it, I suspected there would be some special soap inside – and I was right.

I love such gifts, but this particular one seemed almost too good to use. For quite a while, it stayed on my desk so I could open it and enjoy its beautiful perfume from time to time. Then, one day, I noticed some fine, gold lettering on the back of the tin. 'Housed in a collectible tin,' I read. Yes, it was indeed a cute container. 'Each precious soapette is made from a rich vegetable base . . . to create a decadent lather that leaves the skin brilliantly refreshed.' Yes, my skin could definitely do with such refurbishment, I decided.

But it was what I read next that dumbfounded me. There was the word 'DIRECTIONS' in large, capital letters. What special instructions could one possibly need when using soap?

I read on with interest. 'Add water and massage onto body for a creamy lather. Rinse thoroughly with water.' Really? I checked again to ensure there was no hidden gem there I had missed. After all, I might have been washing the wrong way for years. In the end, however, I decided what they had said pretty much covered everything – which basically amounted to 'add water, then rinse'.

I laughed out loud at that point. Who could possibly need such simple directions? Doesn't *everyone* know that? But I soon remembered how cakes

of soap might be a luxury for some people. Perhaps too some households use only liquid soap or gel – perhaps not everyone is old-fashioned like me.

Then I began thinking more deeply about it all. Could there be other instructions in life I laugh at because they seem so simple or straightforward? How often have I jumped in and done something, without bothering to read the directions first? What else might I decide not to read because I think it will be a waste of time?

After a while, I realised that is exactly how I can be tempted to treat God's word. I can skim over so much, thinking I know all the wisdom it contains. Of course, I believe it and try to live the way I am encouraged to live. But sometimes I hear God saying gently to me, 'Are you hearing me, Jo-Anne? Are you *really* putting into practice the things I am asking you to do here?'

I know too that I need to take to heart the following strong challenge from James:

Do not merely listen to the word, and so deceive yourselves. Do what it says. Anyone who listens to the word but does not do what it says is like someone who looks at his face in a mirror and, after looking at himself, goes away and immediately forgets what he looks like. But whoever looks intently into the perfect law that gives freedom and continues in it – not forgetting what they have heard but doing it – they will be blessed in what they do.

James 1:22–5

May we read the directions in God's word carefully, however simple or familiar they seem. Then may we in fact do what they say.

On Honouring and Serving God

Our Very Best

There we were, our youngest granddaughter and I, chilling out together on a beautiful, sunny day. She had come to visit, complete with her pink, plastic, three-wheeled scooter, and we had decided to explore the nearby paths together. She was only three, so I was genuinely surprised at how she managed to stay upright and keep heading in the right direction.

'Wow, that's excellent,' I told her. 'You ride your scooter so well.'

'I can only do my very best,' she replied in such a cute, matter-of-fact way.

'Pardon?' I said, taken aback.

'I can only do my very best,' she repeated in a most satisfied tone.

I was more than a little impressed. Where had she learnt such wisdom at her age? From her parents? Her teachers at day care? One of her little friends? Some TV programme or other? I could only guess – but I knew she had definitely not learnt it from me.

You see, as I grew up, I think I developed a rather warped idea of what doing my very best meant. I remember how my parents encouraged me to complete my homework, do my piano practice, keep my room tidy, clear the table after meals and fulfil various other commitments as well as I possibly could. But somewhere along the line, I managed to decide that doing my very best was not enough. Instead, I wanted to be *the* best. I needed to beat all those other children in my primary school class when it came to our term exams. I *had* to come top. At high school, I *had* to be on the prize-winners' list each year. I needed to get honours each year too in

On Honouring and Serving God

both my practical and theory piano exams. In short, I became an all-round perfectionist.

While I believe there are pluses in aiming high, even perhaps for perfection, there are downsides. We can become too hard on ourselves. We can become perennially dissatisfied with our efforts. We can end up unable to enjoy any of our excellent achievements. As well, we can become far too hard on those around us as we put our own expectations onto them. What a joy then to hear how our granddaughter had already grasped the concept of doing one's very best and being content with that.

Some of you, like me, might have grown up often hearing the statement, 'If a thing's worth doing, it's worth doing well.' Yet, over the years, I have decided I much prefer the words of Paul in Colossians 3:23–4: 'Whatever you do, work at it with all your heart, as working for the Lord, not for human masters, since you know that you will receive an inheritance from the Lord as a reward. It is the Lord Christ you are serving.'

I prefer these because I now know the Lord Christ whom Paul wrote about. I have experienced his amazing heart of love, his grace, his forgiveness, his understanding. Truly, he deserves our very best. Yet whatever happens, I know he will accept me. His yoke is easy and his burden is light, as the Lord himself has told us (Matthew 11:30) – and I know he will strengthen me and help me grow as I seek to serve him.

Surely that is the best news any perfectionist could ever hear.

On Honouring and Serving God

Just an Old Book?

I hope I never cease to be moved by the amazing life stories I hear, often from the most unexpected people. One such story inspired me to write my first novel, and others have found their way into my more recent books – although it is often these very parts that some readers believe I must have made up. 'Surely that could never happen,' one sceptical lady once told me to my face. Yes, truth can indeed be stranger than fiction at times.

A few months ago, I heard an amazing true story some might well have thought was fiction at a church where I spoke. While chatting with a man there, I discovered he was from South America. When I asked him how he had come to know God, his face lit up and, with great enthusiasm, he launched into his story.

He told me his uncle had belonged to the army in his homeland and, in that role, had been involved in an ongoing war with a neighbouring country. Eventually, their army won a certain battle, which gave all their soldiers the opportunity to raid the nearby town and take whatever they could find for themselves. By the time his uncle made it there, however, the only thing left was an old book.

'What use is that to me?' he thought in disgust. 'But I have some free time now. I might as well start reading it.'

This book turned out to be a Bible. As he read, he wondered if it was true and decided to show it to a Catholic priest in his hometown.

'You shouldn't be reading this,' the priest said, horrified. 'We're the only ones allowed to do that. Give it to me!'

But the uncle refused and eventually found a pastor who explained to him what his Bible was all about. As a result, the uncle soon became a believer.

Yet that was not the end of the story. Eventually, the uncle told his sister about his Bible and about Jesus Christ, and she became a strong believer too. Then, in time, this sister told her son, who also put his faith in Jesus – and this son was the man I met at church that Sunday. Now he takes great pains to tell his own children about God's precious book, the Bible – the word of God that is still so powerful and active today.

When this man's uncle first picked up that old book in the town they had raided, he did not know it was actually a much stronger weapon than any gun or grenade or knife he had as a soldier – or doubled-edged sword, for that matter: 'For the word of God is alive and active. Sharper than any double-edged sword, it penetrates even to dividing soul and spirit, joints and marrow; it judges the thoughts and attitudes of the heart' (Hebrews 4:12). Yet despite his ignorance, God spoke truth deep into the uncle's spirit through its tattered pages – and, thankfully, he had an open, seeker's heart that heard God's call and responded in true belief and faithful obedience.

What an amazing story – and what a challenge to us today as well. May our hearts be equally open to God, and may we always truly value our own 'old book' too as much as the uncle did.

On Honouring and Serving God

Two Coats

I have written several novels which hopefully feature inspiring heroines, but I have decided I do not need to look far to find *real* heroines who are much more worthy of that title. Mostly, they see themselves as ordinary people doing nothing special. Yet their courage in the face of great difficulty is truly inspiring to me.

I think of one such person, a friend from years ago. Back then, both our families had great hopes and plans for the future, yet my friend's journey unfolded in a way she – and we – would never ever have envisaged or hoped for. You see, after some years, certain decisions her husband made and acted upon tore the family apart, causing them all immense grief and pain.

The husband soon decided to marry someone else and my friend was left to care for her children alone, even while dealing with her own grief. She had always been a hard worker, but now redoubled her efforts to provide for the family. After some years, she managed to put a deposit down on an old cottage and continued working at whatever job she could get, often fitting two or three into one day. Eventually both children left home, although one needed constant support as a result of past emotional trauma. At one stage, my friend took in a refugee family, helping to get them on their feet. Then, just as she thought she might slow down a little, she had to pay for expensive repairs to her home, almost losing it to the bank in the process. Soon after, she also needed to provide shelter for her daughter and grandchild after a relationship breakdown.

Now nearing retirement age, she is desperately tired but needs to continue working. As we talked recently, I found myself wishing I had a few

On Loving and Serving Others

thousand dollars to spare to help lift my friend's burden. Yet she was not complaining – in fact, quite the opposite. I tried to tell her she deserved not just one medal but many, yet she disagreed.

'What else can you do?' she said in a matter-of-fact voice. 'You just get on with it.'

She talked then about how thankful she feels and how hard it is for so many others such as the homeless, sleeping on the streets – and it was then that her words touched me most.

'You know, when I see these people, I wish I could help. I often say to Jesus, "But I have *two* coats!" He knows I need them for my work though.'

Two coats, I think to myself. I have so much more than my friend, yet she feels greedy having *two coats*. She has learnt to go on loving, despite life's knocks, and continues to have a soft, merciful heart towards others that surely must delight God's own heart. Her attitude has challenged me deeply, as do the following words of Scripture:

If anyone has material possessions and sees a brother or sister in need but has no pity on them, how can the love of God be in that person? Dear children, let us not love with words or speech but with actions and in truth.
1 John 3:17–18

May God enable us to follow my friend's example, truly care for others and generously share our coats – or anything else we own – with them.

On Loving and Serving Others

Family

Some years ago, a special funeral was held at our church for an elderly man whose only living relative was a sister in the USA. He was a quiet, unassuming gentleman who had served with a Christian organisation in different parts of the world. Each Sunday, he would catch two buses to our church from his home a few suburbs away. But one Sunday, he apparently fell over at home while getting ready, and it was two or three days before friends or neighbours realised something must be wrong. The police broke in and found him, and he was taken to hospital.

As soon as our church heard about his plight, various people started visiting him. Some helped by getting things he needed from home. Others washed his clothes. Still others prayed for and with him. Our pastors liaised with medical staff and kept his sister informed. Then, when the difficult decision had to be made to turn off his life-support system, his Christian friends gathered around his bed, surrounded him in prayer and farewelled him in a most wonderful, godly, dignified way.

At one stage, a nurse commented how sad it was that no family members could be with him at the end of his life.

'But we *are* his family – we're his church family,' those who were present explained.

Perhaps most moving of all, however, were the words of the head ICU doctor who had noted the love, care and respect those who visited had shown to his patient.

On Loving and Serving Others

'I've never seen anything like it,' he told them with feeling.

That was both a wonderful and a sad comment, don't you think? It was wonderful that the sincere, Christlike care given to this elderly gentleman seemed to amaze the doctor, but sad too that he had never before seen people who were not biological family acting in such a loving, caring way. Perhaps he may have come from a culture where these tasks are shouldered by family members only. Who knows? Yet what a reminder to us all of the importance of caring for those alone and in need, not only for their own sake but also for any who might watch on and wonder.

For me, it was a sobering reminder too of Jesus' words in Matthew 25 about gathering the nations together, with the sheep on the right and the goats on the left, then welcoming those on the right to take their kingdom inheritance. The reason Jesus gives for welcoming them is that they helped him when he was hungry and thirsty, in need of clothes and shelter, ill or in prison. He goes on to explain how the hypocrites who consider themselves righteous will argue that they never saw him in such situations – but then adds some words that always cut me to the heart: 'The King will reply, "Truly I tell you, whatever you did for one of the least of these brothers and sisters of mine, you did for me"' (Matthew 25:40).

How thankful I am that that elderly gentleman, who was surely one of Jesus' brothers, with no biological family close by, had his church family around him who treated him in a way that honoured both Jesus and him. May we have the grace to follow their example, showing that same love and being true family to others.

On Loving and Serving Others

The Things We Bring

One cold, rainy afternoon, we drove into the courtyard of a gracious, old bed-and-breakfast (B&B) place, where we had arranged to stay for two nights. The owner, a well-dressed, older woman, greeted us and proceeded to give us a guided tour. As we chatted, she told us about a couple who had planned to stay there on another occasion. Because they had booked late via an online site, she did not know they were coming and had gone out for the day. As soon as she arrived home, however, she found herself well and truly accosted.

'We've been waiting for *five minutes*!' the female would-be guest said angrily. 'This is no way to run a business.'

According to our host, it went downhill from there. The angry woman continued to complain until our host had had enough and refused to allow them to stay.

'But I've paid!' the woman objected.

'Oh no, you haven't,' our host told her firmly. 'I have not authorised the site where you booked to accept payments on my behalf – my guests pay me when they arrive here. This is *my* home and I don't need to let your anger inside here. Goodbye.' With that, she closed the door in their faces.

I immediately had visions of this couple vainly trying to find somewhere else to stay that night, yet I suppose our host had every right to deny them entry. After all, why should she feel obliged to let such an angry spirit affect the peaceful environment she had created in her beautiful B&B?

On Loving and Serving Others

At that point, I decided to reassure her we at least were not about to be angry guests. 'Well, we certainly hope we bring joy and peace with us into your home rather than anger,' I told her.

I would like to have said more, but our host had to rush off. However, as I relaxed in our lovely accommodation, this story kept buzzing around in my mind and I began to wonder what sort of baggage I myself carry with me into the various places I enter. As a child of God, I have God's Spirit in me, so hopefully others can see something at least of the grace of God present in me. Hopefully too, some of the fruits of the Spirit – love, joy, peace, patience, kindness, goodness, faithfulness, gentleness and self-control – will be evident in the way I treat others and the words I choose to say. Yet surely there have been many times when I have entered someone's home or workplace with anger . . . or judgement . . . or plain old grumpiness in my heart?

It is a sobering thought that we have been entrusted with carrying God's peace wherever we go and sharing it with others, as in the beautiful blessing below. We can choose to open our hearts and do this with joy and love – or we can close them and, in the process, add to others' burdens. We can bless or we can curse. The choice is ours.

May God help us all to choose rightly.

The LORD bless you
  and keep you;
the LORD make his face shine on you
  and be gracious to you;
the LORD turn his face towards you
  and give you peace.

Numbers 6:24–6

On Loving and Serving Others

An Important Question

I had finished my grocery shopping and went to join the shortest check-out queue when I noticed a man heading the same way.

'Ladies before gentlemen,' he said with a smile.

As I thanked him and forged on, I bumped my trolley against the counter. 'Oops – I can't seem to see where I'm going,' I laughed.

'I've been trying to work that out for the past seventy years!' he quickly replied.

My mind whirred as I stacked my groceries on the counter, but before I could respond, he spoke again. 'Do *you* know where you're going?'

For a moment, his question seemed to hang in the air between us. It was as if time stood still – and as if God was saying gently to me, 'Well, Jo-Anne – speak up!'

At that point, I blurted out the first thing that came to mind. 'Actually, I *do* know where I'm going.'

'Oh, where's that?' he responded.

'Well, I know I belong to God – I love Jesus and I believe I'm going to heaven.'

He looked slightly taken aback but then began sharing a little poem with me that I recognised at the time. When he had finished, I decided that, if he could quote something to me, I could perhaps quote something back.

On Loving and Serving Others

'Oh, I love 1 John 3:1: "See what great love the Father has lavished on us, that we should be called children of God! And that is what we are!" It's amazing we can be called children of God, don't you think?'

After a slight pause, he then dredged up a Bible verse of his own from somewhere deep in the recesses of his brain – perhaps from childhood? I could not catch it all but nodded and smiled.

'What's your name?' he demanded then.

'I'm Jo-Anne. What's yours?'

'I'm Tony,' he told me in a lovely European accent.

'Good to chat, Tony,' I replied, realising as I did that the check-out girl was smiling at me and the next customer was looking at me somewhat strangely.

Later, I thought of much better things I could have said instead. Still, at least this gentleman had not seemed put off. In fact, I sensed something had stirred in him as we chatted – perhaps something God had spoken into his heart long ago? Perhaps too our conversation would cause him to reflect a little more on the very question he had asked me. But then I began to wonder if my response may have sounded a little too presumptuous. Even as I had answered him, I remember thinking, 'This could sound so proud and arrogant.' Yet, Scripture clearly talks about the eternal life we know we have through Jesus: 'And this is the testimony: God has given us eternal life, and this life is in his Son. Whoever has the Son has life; whoever does not have the Son of God does not have life' (1 John 5:11–12).

We have been given the wonderful privilege of knowing God's Son and of having him present in our lives here and now, as well as on into eternity. Because of Jesus, we know the answer to this man's question, 'Do you know where you are going?' Surely then, we need to share this good news with others however and wherever we can – even perhaps in shopping queues.

On Loving and Serving Others

What's Your Secret?

It was the second to last day of our wonderful holiday in New Zealand's South Island. We had arrived at the wharf in Picton for our ferry trip to Wellington, only to discover the ferry was cancelled. So . . . what to do in the hours until the next ferry arrived? At that point, I admit I felt more than a little miffed that our plans for our afternoon in Wellington were foiled.

In the end, we visited a nearby museum and also enjoyed a delicious morning tea. Then I noticed a jewellery store that seemed to beckon enticingly to me.

'I'll read in the car,' my husband volunteered, 'but make sure you buy something nice for yourself.'

After wandering around the store for some time, I chose a pretty pair of paua-shell earrings.

'This is part of our Golden Wedding anniversary celebration,' I told the young girl serving me. 'They'll always remind me of our special time in New Zealand.'

'You don't look old enough for a Golden Wedding anniversary,' an older staff member standing nearby commented, smiling.

I told her my age then, all the while thinking what a perfect salesperson she was.

'*No!*' she responded, seemingly shocked. 'Your skin's so smooth – you look much younger than that. What's your secret?'

I laughed and was about to give some flippant answer but felt a check in my spirit. In that moment, I saw my opportunity to say something of more lasting value instead.

On Loving and Serving Others

'Well', I began, 'my husband's been a minister all our married life. We both have a firm faith in God and are keen members of our church. I think when you are at peace inside yourself, that makes a big difference all round, don't you?'

The older lady nodded, round-eyed. 'But what have you yourself done in your life?' she asked then.

I told her briefly about my various occupations, including how I myself had trained for ministry in my forties and become a writer in my late fifties. We talked for a while about how important it is to keep learning and growing in our lives, a concept with which she strongly agreed.

'What books do you write? Do you have a card or something so we can look you up?' the younger girl burst out then.

I explained how my books have a lot of 'faith content', then found two business cards in my bag, hoping and praying both women would indeed look up my website and read about the books I have written.

After chatting a while longer, I reluctantly left, in awe of how God had given me this unexpected, little window of opportunity to share something at least with these women about the difference faith in God can make in our lives. My words were no doubt inadequate, especially since I was still feeling disgruntled that our plans had been changed, yet I hoped and prayed God would still use them.

We have a wonderful 'secret' indeed to share. May we not keep it to ourselves but, instead, endeavour to pass it on with gentleness and grace however and whenever we can.

Always be prepared to give an answer to everyone who asks you to give the reason for the hope that you have. But do this with gentleness and respect.
1 Peter 3:15b

On Loving and Serving Others

Paying It Forward

'I can't believe I'm actually getting a piano,' our daughter commented to us all as we celebrated her birthday together. She had wanted a piano of her own to play for such a long time. There has always been one in our home and, as a child, she had had piano lessons. Then, as a teenager, she had chosen to have more lessons in order to be able to enjoy playing her favourite songs. Soon, however, she moved out of home and eventually married and had children. But from time to time when visiting us, she still loved to sit down and play our old piano.

Then one day, a friend of mine put a post on Facebook, asking if anyone would like her piano as she planned to move house and could not take it with her. At first, I hesitated. I knew our daughter could not afford to pay anything for it – and surely my friend would not be prepared to give it away? Yet that is exactly what happened.

'I just want my piano to go to a good home,' she explained. 'Someone kindly left it to me in her will, so I'd like to pass it on now in the same spirit it was passed on to me.'

Soon a removalist was found and that piano wended its way to our daughter's home, where it fitted perfectly in a corner of her living-room as if it were meant to belong there. After a tuning, it sounded even better and continues to give our daughter much joy.

Soon after this, I witnessed another happy moment when our daughter-in-law gave this same daughter several boxes of pre-loved girls' clothes that our older grandchildren could no longer wear.

On Loving and Serving Others

'That's excellent,' our daughter exclaimed, delighted. 'The other day, my friend passed on some great boys' clothes to us too.'

As it happens, many of these are designer-label clothes that were barely worn and that our daughter could never afford to buy. So once her own children have grown out of them, she will pass them on to other friends who are always grateful to receive them for their children.

Seeing these events unfold in our daughter's life caused me to reflect on what possessions I have that could bless others in some way and how willing I might be to pass them on to others – not only material possessions but also the many spiritual blessings I have received. Sometimes, I suspect I like to cling to things I regard as precious rather than think of others' needs. Sometimes, I can be stingy rather than generous. Sometimes, I can very easily forget how someone else bothered to share the good news of Jesus with me rather than keep it to themselves. Sometimes, I can even forget how freely God's love was showered on me and how this same love now needs to flow on through me to others.

May I always remember the generosity of heart our daughter experienced and pay it forward to others myself however I can with joy and gratitude.

Freely you have received; freely give.

Matthew 10:8b

The world of the generous gets larger and larger;
   the world of the stingy gets smaller and smaller.
The one who blesses others is abundantly blessed;
   those who help others are helped.

Proverbs 11:24–5, MSG

On Loving and Serving Others

The Best Attitude

I wonder if you can think of a time when someone treated you or spoke to you in a way that made you feel truly valued and respected. I am thankful to say I can. But perhaps you have had the opposite experience too, as I have once or twice, when you ended up feeling more than a little used or worthless instead.

Many moons ago, I worked as a casual teacher in various local high schools. Some of these experiences were excellent, but others were far less enjoyable, to say the least. At one school, I asked a girl standing nearby as politely as I could if she would mind moving a chair that was in everyone's way.

'Move it yourself!' she snapped back in a surly manner. 'That's what you're paid to do.'

At another school, after filling in for a few days in the history department, I was asked to stay on longer as they had discovered the teacher I was replacing would be away for some time. Not wanting her classes to get behind, I asked the subject master, whose role, I understood, was to help his staff, for advice on what to teach the classes. I was happy to put in the extra effort required rather than merely babysit them but, since I usually taught languages, I felt a little at sea.

'Work it out yourself!' he responded in an angry, abrupt way. 'That's what you're paid for.'

In the end, I did. But I also eventually reported him to the principal and never returned to the history department of that school.

On Loving and Serving Others

On the other hand, I have experienced many other wonderful moments when I have felt greatly valued and respected. I think of one occasion years ago when I was invited to speak at a well-attended women's breakfast. From the outset, I felt honoured and cared for. Someone volunteered to sell my books on my behalf so I could focus on speaking. There was a prayer team ready to pray alongside me for anyone afterwards. Later I discovered this church had also given me what I felt was an embarrassingly generous monetary gift for coming and speaking.

Then not long ago, I came away from an online interview with a potential publisher feeling truly respected and taken seriously. Later I realised why. My interviewer had listened carefully to me, had given me time to ask my own questions and, in general, had treated me in a polite and professional manner. What a joy!

Recently, I noticed a simple, pithy, little statement in one of Peter's letters to the early believers that, while directed at Christian slaves, surely applies to us all today too:

Show proper respect to everyone.

1 Peter 2:17a

No, this is not a command for us to rush to do everyone's bidding or let others ride roughshod over us. Instead, it should remind us to see others, whoever they are and whether we like or agree with them or not, as human beings created in the image of God, as those loved by God equally as much as we are, as those who have gifts to offer, as those who may well long to feel honoured, respected and loved too.

Surely this is the best attitude for us all to have as we walk this earth together?

On Loving and Serving Others

Sensing Those 'Isms'

I watched as our salesperson went to ask a male colleague nearby a question on our behalf. We were making an important purchase – a new car – and had several queries.

'No, that's wrong,' her male colleague said loudly, frowning. 'Don't you *remember*? You take that amount *off*.'

I felt sorry for our salesperson and, when she returned, pretended I had not heard. Soon after, she decided to double-check something else, this time with her senior manager. A moment later, he strode across and took over from her.

'I'm not sure where she was up to,' he said with a disapproving expression as he looked at her paperwork. 'I thought she would've explained this to you already.'

I did not warm to his slick, arrogant tone and again felt sorry for our salesperson who had done her best. As he talked, she stood in the background, looking as if she might have preferred to be invisible.

I was sure I had detected more than a touch of blatant sexism in these two exchanges. Our salesperson had been doing well and I felt her male colleagues had put her down in a very public way. Yet the previous day, I had noticed hints of a different sort of 'ism' in this same salesperson's own response when we told her we wanted to go away and think about our options.

'Well, you can do that,' she told us. 'But don't leave it too long or you're likely to forget all the things I've told you today.'

On Loving and Serving Others

Was I being supersensitive? Possibly. Yet this was not the only whiff of ageism I sensed while ordering our new car. When we went to pay our deposit the next day, we were ushered into a nearby office.

'Are you comfortable with transferring money online or would you prefer to pay by bank cheque?' the girl asked us politely, unaware, I am sure, how condescending she sounded.

My husband smiled and told her that transferring money online would be fine, thank you. I felt like adding the words 'despite how elderly and decrepit we might look' but managed to restrain myself just in time.

We can all judge others so easily – just as I may have already done in what I have written here. We like putting people in boxes. Some of us assume women are too illogical and feather-brained for this or that role. Some of us assume all elderly people lack certain abilities. Some of us assume so much about people from different ethnic and cultural backgrounds. We may not mean our comments to sound patronising or judgemental – quite the opposite, in fact. Yet, perhaps taking a little more thought and care before blurting things out would be much more helpful and respectful.

Maybe too we all need to reflect more on Jesus' strong words about judging others: 'Don't pick on people, jump on their failures, criticize their faults – unless, of course, you want the same treatment. That critical spirit has a way of boomeranging. It's easy to see a smudge on your neighbor's face and be oblivious to the ugly sneer on your own' (Matthew 7:1–3, MSG).

I hope we can soon become much more oblivious to those smudges on others' faces. After all, God has looked past the many smudges on our own – and still does.

On Loving and Serving Others

Precious Lessons from Life's Painful Times

It is probably safe to say that most of us try to avoid pain as much as possible. It is unpleasant. It can restrict our activities. It can dull our enjoyment of life and . . . well, it hurts – a lot.

At one stage when I had severe lower-back and leg pain for several weeks, a friend sent me a beautiful card. Inside, she had written how she hoped I would soon be pain-free and urged me to let her know if there was any way she could help. Her kind words moved me – and I knew she meant them. This friend is always so sensitive to others' needs, reaching out to help however she can.

One reason for this, I suspect, is that she herself knows what pain is like. Not long before this, two close family members had passed away, one in tragic circumstances. Another family member suffers severe ongoing health issues and, on top of this, she herself is often in physical pain. Naturally speaking, she would be the last person one would expect to have either the physical or emotional resources to care so sacrificially for others. Yet from God's perspective, she has exactly what it takes. To me, she epitomises Paul's words:

Praise be to the God and Father of our Lord Jesus Christ, the Father of compassion and the God of all comfort, who comforts us in all our troubles, so that we can comfort those in any trouble with the comfort we ourselves receive from God.
2 Corinthians 1:3–4

Unlike my friend, I had not faced anywhere near the same sad events and debilitating illnesses. I had had severe back and leg pain before, but this had eventually passed. This time, however, my pain seemed more serious

On Loving and Serving Others

and persistent. I was on medication. I used hot packs on my lower back. I did what exercises I could and saw a physiotherapist. I prayed for healing and others did too. But still the pain persisted.

What did I learn through it all? What good did God bring out of this time for me – and hopefully others? I believe it gave me a small glimpse at least into what life must be like for those who suffer all the time from chronic, physical pain – and my heart goes out to them. I understand now how this could colour their whole experience of life and cause them to feel quite alienated and removed from those around them. I can also appreciate much more what an effort it must be for them to participate in those normal, everyday activities we so often take for granted.

It was too late at that point for me to empathise with my father, who suffered from severe, chronic sciatica for as long as I can remember. Yet I believe I now understand at least one of the reasons he was often so short-tempered with others and somewhat withdrawn, unable to enjoy life to the full. But it is not too late for me to do better at understanding and empathising with others around me now.

Have you, like me, learnt some important lessons through the hard things of life? May God use your painful experiences to bring comfort to others too, in whatever way is right for you.

On Loving and Serving Others

Listening Well

My daughter and I sat on her back patio in the warm sun, chatting as we ate our lunch. My husband and I had already celebrated Mother's Day with our son's family on the day itself and enjoyed a delicious afternoon tea together, but I had decided I wanted to catch up with our two daughters separately at a later date. This then was my opportunity to spend time with our older daughter and, to me, those special moments we enjoyed together were priceless.

I had made egg sandwiches, which our daughter then garnished with parsley and chives from her garden, thus adding a wonderful aroma and taste that elevated my basic fare above the ordinary. Then she served a delicious sponge cake she had baked, complete with jam and cream in the centre and icing sugar on top. What a treat! Immediately, it brought back comforting memories of my mother's and grandmother's sponges which I myself have never been able to replicate.

We topped off our modest yet special lunch with hot cups of tea, so enjoyable in themselves. But as we relaxed and chatted, I was reminded again of something I have noticed many times in the past and also experienced myself, which is simply this. Most of us long so much to be listened to. *Really* listened to, that is. This day with our daughter, I felt truly heard as I aired my current concerns about my writing and life in general with her. I hope and pray she felt the same too as I tried my best to hear clearly the things she shared and empathise with her in the process.

On Loving and Serving Others

You see, one thing she mentioned during this time was that, when talking with certain of her friends, she often does not feel truly heard. 'They just do not *listen*!' she told me with great frustration.

Have you ever experienced this yourself? This is how misunderstandings happen, isn't it? We can feel negated and disrespected and . . . well, plain wrong. We can also come to believe that what we have to offer the world is somehow worthless.

Sadly, I suspect I am aware of this issue because I myself tend to talk a lot in a one-on-one setting. I have so many thoughts and ideas running around in my head that I know I can easily monopolise a conversation and even silence the other person at times. This can be particularly damaging when someone has come specifically to meet with me for support and prayer. In these instances, it is even more essential that *I* listen to *them*, rather than vice versa. I need to give them space, honour who they are and, in general, hear them well. I need to rein in my own desires and, instead, put the other person first.

One verse of Scripture that has challenged me often in this area:

To answer before listening –
   that is folly and shame.

Proverbs 18:13

In *The Message* version, Eugene Peterson puts it even more bluntly: 'Answering before listening is both stupid and rude.' Ouch! I do not like to think of myself as stupid or rude, yet I am sure those adjectives describe me well whenever I rush in and respond too early.

May we all learn to close our mouths more often and listen well instead.

On Loving and Serving Others

Reckless Words

They can slide off our tongues before we know it. Perhaps they are spoken in a burst of anger or irritation – or perhaps they slip out in a thoughtless moment when our minds are elsewhere. Whatever the case, our reckless words can leave their mark for a very long time as can the reckless words others might say to us.

Recently, I listened, heart in mouth, as someone made a brief remark to another that was meant to be polite and kind. Unfortunately, the one speaking had forgotten how much the other person hated such comments. A moment later, I observed the facial expressions of both change. The person who had spoken looked horrified and remorseful as if they would give anything to take their words back, while the other looked more than a little angry and offended.

Immediately, I felt sorry for them both. I tried my best to smooth things over and change the topic of conversation but was only partially successful. The words had been said and the damage had been done.

Sometimes, however, we may speak to wound others on purpose. I still remember clearly an occasion years ago when I spoke rashly in anger, unconcerned at how hurtful my words might be to the person at whom they were aimed. In that instant, all I wanted to do was to lash out, determined to defend myself and get my point across. Later, I deeply regretted it, although my opinion on the matter under discussion did not change. I apologised – and so did the other person involved – but significant ground was lost in the process and, sadly, there was little opportunity later to restore the relationship and establish trust again between us.

On Loving and Serving Others

No wonder the following verse resonated deeply with me soon after – and still does:

The words of the reckless pierce like swords,
but the tongue of the wise brings healing.

Proverbs 12:18

I long for the words that roll off my tongue to bring true healing rather than piercing pain to others, don't you? On occasions, we do need to speak firmly and with passion, to stand up for what is right and not let things slide because we lack the courage to confront. In those instances, it will hopefully be righteous anger and the desire for God's justice to rule that motivate us. But at all times, our goal needs to be restoration and healing – for others and for ourselves.

Further on in the same chapter, we find the following:

Anxiety weighs down the heart,
but a kind word cheers it up.

Proverbs 12:25

We are often unaware what others are going through or what is driving them to act the way they do. At times, we can see anxiety written on a person's face or observe it in their words and actions. Yet many of us are adept at burying such emotions well below the surface so that others will not notice. How important it is then to speak in a kind manner because those few words from us can lighten another's load in ways we might never imagine.

Love is patient, love is kind. It does not envy, it does not boast, it is not proud.
1 Corinthians 13:4

Be kind and compassionate to one another, forgiving each other, just as in Christ God forgave you.

Ephesians 4:32

On Loving and Serving Others

Let There Be Light

In our home, I have a reputation for liking to let as much light in as possible. Each morning, the first thing I do is raise the blind on our bedroom windows. Then I open the curtains in our dining area and the shutters on our kitchen window. Finally, I pull the blind up in my study. Usually, my husband has already opened the curtains across the doors leading onto our balcony so I can see the sky and trees outside. But, because we live in a downstairs unit, I often like some electric lights on as well, especially in dull weather.

There is something attractive about light, isn't there? A few weeks ago, when the smoke from various bushfires not far from our home finally cleared, many of us felt so happy to see sunlight and blue sky again. Somehow, natural light seems to lift our spirits and have a truly positive effect on our wellbeing. But light is so useful too in all its various shapes and forms. Without it, we can lose direction, stumble over things and, in general, be unable to function to the best of our ability.

Light is attractive. Light is useful – and light can even save us too. Just think of those lighthouses that have prevented so many ships from floundering on dangerous rocks.

One Saturday at our church, we held a women's retreat focused on the theme, 'Let there be light!' Everything was set out beautifully, with fairy lights strung here and there and little artificial candles on our tables that we were all invited to switch on at one stage. But two beautiful collections of lights at the front of our auditorium caught my attention in particular, each made up of a fascinating mix of small and large lamps, along with candles

of all shapes and sizes in intricate candleholders. As the day unfolded, one after the other, all these beautiful lamps and candles were gradually lit to reflect the fact that each of us is called to be a light to our world, whatever our 'shape' or however we are equipped to shine. As we receive God's grace and mercy and step from darkness to light ourselves, we have the wonderful privilege of belonging to God and being chosen to show God's goodness to the world so that others may also be drawn towards that light:

. . . for you are a chosen people. You are royal priests, a holy nation, God's very own possession. As a result, you can show others the goodness of God, for he called you out of the darkness into his wonderful light.

1 Peter 2:9, NLT

At one point that day, I saw in my mind a picture of a huge throng of women, each carrying a light high as they streamed from all corners of the world towards a beautiful, shining throne surrounded by light. I was overwhelmed at the privilege of being counted among that throng and being able to hold my own lamp high as we praised God together. What a wonderful day that will be for us all when this happens in reality!

May we each in our own unique way allow God's light to shine through us in all we do and say, so that others may find their way to God too.

On Loving and Serving Others

A Lesson in Tenacity

Whenever it rained heavily, we knew the creek at the back of our old house could inundate our yard. After all, this creek flows down from a tall ridge and, when heavy rains coincide with a high tide in the nearby river, all that water has to go somewhere. So here we were again, watching that murky creek rapidly rise. Our house itself was in no danger, but our hearts sank as we remembered the mess previous floods left behind. We did not look forward to all that shovelling, hosing and cleaning up yet again.

Then I noticed that a blueberry ash tree I had planted several years earlier on the creek bank was surrounded by swirling water. I had found this tree at our local council's 'free tree' day when it was only a tiny seedling and, somehow, it had already managed to survive an attack from our lawnmower, as well as total lack of care in general. Now it was still standing upright, despite the muddy water around it – and, for some reason, I felt so proud of it.

I left my post momentarily and, when I returned, my blueberry ash was nowhere to be seen. I stood staring at the spot, feeling sad for a tree that had fought so bravely to survive. It had cost me nothing so was no great loss but it had taken years to get to about a metre and half in height.

Not long after, my husband ventured down our yard to begin cleaning up – and, next time I looked, there was my blueberry ash again!

'A pile of debris had caught in its leaves and weighed it down,' he told me. 'Once I removed it all, the tree sprang back up.'

On Faithfulness and Perseverance

Later, I went down to inspect my tree myself. Yes, it was standing upright, albeit at a slight angle. Even its dark blue berries were still intact. At its base, the roots had obviously been tested but had held firm. I straightened my tree, packed more earth around the roots and placed a rock at its base. Hopefully, it would survive and grow even firmer and stronger.

As I worked, I thought of some words from Psalm 1:

Blessed is the one
   who does not walk in step with the wicked
or stand in the way that sinners take
   or sit in the company of mockers,
but whose delight is in the law of the LORD,
   and who meditates on his law day and night.
That person is like a tree planted by streams of water,
   which yields its fruit in season
and whose leaf does not wither –
   whatever they do prospers.

Psalm 1:1–3

The roots of my blueberry ash had obviously gone down deep enough into the moist soil by the creek to withstand the fast-flowing flood waters. Yes, my tree had been weighed down with debris but had stood firm. What a graphic reminder to me to close my ears to the 'debris' of doubt and discouragement and, instead, send my roots down deep into the word of God, drinking from that life-giving water only God can provide. Then, when difficulties threaten to overwhelm, I can remain unmoved, shake myself off and keep going.

May you too be like my blueberry ash, standing firm, however deep and murky the waters around you may become.

On Faithfulness and Perseverance

Being a Child Again

I was glad no one else could see me. There I was in my kitchen, kneading my latest batch of home-made playdough into a lovely, squishy ball. I had coloured it bright blue for our grandson and knew I should put it in a container to keep it from drying out. But surely I could keep playing with it for a while . . . couldn't I?

Later, I went to look through some cute toys our older granddaughters had lent to us for their younger cousins to play with and decided they needed slow and careful sorting . . . didn't they? I soon found a whole playground to assemble, complete with little, pretend children in cars and on swings and tiny tricycles. Next, in a large box, I discovered something called an 'imaginarium', a miniature wooden village with train tracks leading here and there and a little pink train with carriages that joined together via magnets, along with some tiny cars, people and trees. Then I came across a weird-looking 'Mr Potato Head', with a selection of eyes, noses, arms and legs ready to be firmly attached.

I had so much fun sorting and playing with all these interesting toys. I ignored all the other tasks awaiting my attention and thoroughly enjoyed my stolen moments of play. There were no grandchildren around to interrupt me and want whatever I had – and no grown-up children around to laugh and shake their heads at their mother. In fact, there were no other adults nearby at all to wonder at what I was doing – and perhaps even be a little jealous?

On Faithfulness and Perseverance

Was it a waste of time? Definitely not. In the midst of my play, a response Jesus once gave to a question about who would be greatest in the kingdom of heaven came to mind:

Truly I tell you, unless you change and become like little children, you will never enter the kingdom of heaven.

Matthew 18:3

I have been a Christian for a long time. Yet I still need to hold on to the sort of childlike faith that trusts our heavenly Father implicitly. I need to recognise his voice and listen to what he says. I need to talk with him, and laugh and cry with him – and perhaps even play with him a little. Maybe then, I will become more like him.

Recently, I read again the story of Zacchaeus in Luke 19. Zacchaeus was a wealthy, important, grown man. Yet he was so eager to see Jesus that he did something quite childish. He climbed a tree to get a better view. Imagine how he felt when Jesus stopped right under that tree, called him by name and informed him he planned to come to his home. At once, Zacchaeus scrambled down from that tree in full view of everyone and welcomed Jesus into his life. The result? 'Jesus said to him, "Today salvation has come to this house, because this man, too, is a son of Abraham"' (Luke 19:9).

I might have difficulty climbing trees these days but I hope that, like Zacchaeus, I will always be prepared to do whatever it takes to see Jesus more clearly. I hope I can continue to have the childlike faith that keeps trusting him, whatever happens – and I hope you can too.

On Faithfulness and Perseverance

Gone

One morning it was there. By night-time, it was gone. We had been warned this would happen, but it was still a shock. How could they do such a thing?

For around thirty years, the humble, red-brick home with the neat yard had sat across the road from our house. But then the elderly lady who owned it passed away and it was sold. The new owners told us they planned to demolish it and build a large, two-storey one in its place and, sure enough, some months later, wire fences were erected around the old house. Soon the brick veneer and building material containing asbestos were carefully removed, leaving the bones of the old house exposed for all to see. A huge excavator took up residence in the front yard and sat there idle for a few days. Then, early one morning, trucks began arriving and the excavator went into action.

By the evening, the house had been levelled. The following day, more trucks arrived to take away the rubbish, leaving nothing remaining of what was once such a neat, comfortable, old home.

I watched all this happen with some sadness. I understood that the owners needed a bigger house, given they had three small children. But to me it seemed that, with every brick that was removed from the old home, part of the life of the elderly lady who used to live there went with it. I remembered her gentle husband as well and how they seemed so devoted to each other. They had no children, they told us once, and planned to leave the home to a disabled nephew to provide for his future care. Yet now, all trace of this lovely couple had been obliterated.

On Faithfulness and Perseverance

As well as bringing sadness, however, this event also served as a sober reminder to me that one day, those material things we cling to so tightly in this world will all disappear. One day, whether our home is a massive mansion or a tumbledown shack, it will crumble and disappear – and who can tell what will happen to any other material possessions we may leave behind?

Even as I was thinking about this, I began reading the next psalm I was up to in my Bible. Imagine my surprise when I came to the following:

Show me, Lord, my life's end
   and the number of my days;
   let me know how fleeting my life is.
You have made my days a mere handbreadth;
   the span of my years is as nothing before you.
Everyone is but a breath,
   even those who seem secure.
Surely everyone goes around like a mere phantom;
   in vain they rush about, heaping up wealth
   without knowing whose it will finally be.

Psalm 39:4–6

I do not really care what happens to our home after we are gone. But I *do* care whether the things I am pouring my energies into right now will make an impact that will last for eternity. I want my treasure to be in heaven where it cannot be destroyed rather than here where bulldozers can demolish it in a day.

May we all learn to live with eternity in mind. May we always seek to build God's kingdom rather than our own as we remember well how fleeting our earthly lives truly are.

On Faithfulness and Perseverance

A Jarring Wake-up Call

When our phone rang very early one Sunday morning, we knew it could not be good news. One of our daughters was calling to tell us that their unit had been broken into during the night while they were asleep. Lots of things were stolen, including TV, laptop, mobile phones, wedding ring, handbag, wallet and keys to their unit, cars and workplaces. As well, the family had no household insurance cover.

Where to start in dealing with such an event? The police had already been called, but now, in a hurry, they needed to find out how to cancel credit cards. Next, they had to track down a locksmith to change the locks. A few days later, they discovered more things had been taken than they had thought, which involved more paperwork and more running around to fix up this and that.

Our daughter and her husband were not well off and had two small children. They were a struggling young family with a large mortgage, trying to meet all their financial obligations in life. On top of that, our son-in-law was studying in his spare time. Yes, they both had jobs but were not highly paid, so anything they owned was hard won. But when they were robbed, while they were aghast at what they had lost and their minds reeled at the thought of how they could afford to replace everything, they both came to the same conclusion. What they had lost was only 'stuff'. Yes, it was important 'stuff', but they were all safe – and that was the main thing. Soon after, they discovered a large carving knife was missing too. If they had come out into the living area when things were being taken, who knows what could have happened?

On Faithfulness and Perseverance

Through this whole unpleasant experience, we saw what a difference the generosity of others could make. Some offered the loan or gift of a mobile phone. Some brought meals. Others gave money. One family even delivered a spare TV to them. There is nothing like people helping people, showing God's love via practical help, is there? Each in their own way, these folk too have realised the importance of relationship with others over hanging on to material possessions.

Truly, the material things around us are so temporary. One day we have them – the next, they may all be gone. How much more easily our family can now relate to Jesus' words:

Do not store up for yourselves treasures on earth, where moths and vermin destroy, and where thieves break in and steal. But store up for yourselves treasures in heaven, where moths and vermin do not destroy, and where thieves do not break in and steal. For where your treasure is, there your heart will be also.

Matthew 6:19–21

I am so glad there will be no jarring wake-up call to tell us those unseen heavenly treasures have gone missing. God has promised they are eternal and will be there, waiting for us. How blessed we are that we can set our hearts on these things rather than anything the world could ever offer us.

So we fix our eyes not on what is seen, but on what is unseen, since what is seen is temporary, but what is unseen is eternal.

2 Corinthians 4:18

On Faithfulness and Perseverance

Upside-down Olympics

I often have mixed feelings when watching the Olympic Games. Part of me revels in it all, rejoicing in the successes the competitors experience and admiring their fine-honed skills. I am no sportswoman but I love seeing excellence in action as I watch the swimming, gymnastics, rowing, cycling and track-and-field events. I admire the highly committed athletes who have persevered and excelled in their chosen sport. They have spent countless hours working hard, no doubt training when they did not feel like it, and perhaps making huge financial sacrifices in the process. No wonder they have their eyes on the prize and want to win.

But another part of me feels sad when someone is beaten, often by a tiny margin. Surely they are still amazing athletes whether they came first or second or third – or nowhere? I often feel a little annoyed when commentators focus only on the medal winners and relegate other competitors to the background. I also feel relieved when I hear a competitor say, with apparent honesty, that they are just glad to be part of it all, that they are delighted with their silver or bronze medal and that they are happy to see others, especially their teammates, do better than they have or succeed in winning.

Perhaps I am more like a friend of mine than I thought I was. She refuses to play any competitive games, even Scrabble or Monopoly, because someone has to lose. Or I think of something my husband, who does not appreciate football, once said: 'I don't understand why they don't give each team a ball. It's so unseemly for them both to fight over just one.' A friend told us once that, in a certain country where he used to live, whenever a team from one

village scored a goal in football, they would all agree it was the other team's turn to score the next.

I am so glad being a follower of Jesus is not competitive in any way. In fact, in Matthew 20, Jesus describes a very upside-down approach to the 'game of life' in which we all participate. He tells a story about some men who are hired at different times throughout the day to work in the vineyards. Yet, that evening, they all receive the same wage. When those who worked longer object, the landowner reminds them that they agreed to be paid the amount they received and that he was not being unfair to them. Then he continues: 'Don't I have the right to do what I want with my own money? Or are you envious because I am generous?' (verse 15).

Then comes the most upside-down part of all. Jesus goes on to say to those present: 'So the last will be first, and the first will be last' (verse 16). That would not go down too well in the Olympics, would it? Yes, we are to 'run in such a way as to get the prize' (1 Corinthians 9:24b). But that prize is awarded irrespective of when we join the race and wherever we come as we persevere in fixing our eyes on Jesus (Hebrews 12:1–2).

So, as we all run our race in these upside-down Olympics, may we continue to encourage and spur one another on with generous, loving hearts.

On Faithfulness and Perseverance

Turning the Clock Back

I never thought I would see the day. Yet there I was, sitting in a Latin class once again – and somehow, despite the inordinate number of years since I had last conjugated a Latin verb or thought seriously about Latin declensions, there was a distinct familiarity to it all.

Knowing I was coming to visit from interstate, my sister had asked her U3A (University of the Third Age) teacher if I could attend his Latin class with her. What a blast from the past it was. To my surprise, I was warmly welcomed as some sort of expert simply because I had studied Latin for four years at high school, majored in modern languages at university and also survived a year of classical Greek there. As to how much I remembered . . . well, that was a different matter altogether.

The teacher began by gently helping everyone revise all they had learnt up to that point. As he did, I felt I was in some sort of wind tunnel, being sucked inexorably back over the years. As the beautiful Latin phrases tumbled so effortlessly from his lips, I was again seated in that high-school classroom on a stifling, summer day, listening to my old teacher's raspy voice as she explained some finer point of Latin grammar. I am sure I heard her sigh with exasperation too as she attempted to guide us through Livy's account of Hannibal's battle exploits, then help us appreciate the finer points of Latin poetry as we scanned lines from Virgil's *Aeneid*. We were all so young and restless, eager to get out of the classroom and leave our school days behind.

I returned to the present with a jolt, realising as I did how different my current Latin class experience was – and what a different place I was at

in my life now too. This time around, our teacher was a gracious, retired university lecturer who knew exactly how to explain things well and how to remind everyone gently about what they already knew, without making them feel too stupid. The class members were all mature-age, experienced, lifelong learners who truly valued this opportunity to unravel the intricacies of Latin and put their minds to work again. I went along for the ride, enjoying it all, and did so with a truly thankful heart as I reflected on the journey God has enabled me to take during the time that has elapsed since my high-school Latin days.

My life has involved several unforeseen, interesting twists and turns as I have moved from one career to another over the years. Some roles I undertook would, I thought, perhaps be forever, yet that was not to be. Yet as I look back, I can see how God taught me things in each role that proved so useful in the next, all the while shaping me to become more of the person I was created to be. I suspect I may have made some wrong decisions along the way, yet God has watched over me and guided me through it all. My times have indeed been in God's hands – and I hope you know yours are too.

But I trust in you, Lord;
 I say, 'You are my God.'
My times are in your hands.

Psalm 31:14–15a

On Faithfulness and Perseverance

Forging Ahead

I own an interesting, old sewing machine, a Husqvarna 3610 model I bought way back in the seventies. I used it to make our younger daughter's primary-school unforms and now she is over forty years old. It sat relatively idle for some years after that until I lent it to our older daughter who eventually returned it to me. But alas, I discovered it had developed a slight problem – it seemed determined to sew only backwards! However much I cleaned, oiled and jiggled that reverse button, it stubbornly remained stuck fast.

As I reflected on this problem, I remembered times when I had become stuck in life, unable or unwilling to make certain changes to help me move forward. Sometimes, I did not want to let go of the past or put aside a dream that had little chance of coming to fruition. I was afraid to make a firm decision to move on or launch out in a new direction. I remember thinking at one stage I could never give up high-school teaching because that was what I had studied hard to do. Yet, by God's grace, an opportunity to become an editor of school curriculum material presented itself and my working life took a whole new turn. Not only did I enjoy my editing job but also, unbeknown to me, God was preparing me ahead of time to become the writer I am today.

We can become stuck in our spiritual journeys too – and that to me is even sadder. Sometimes, we power on, growing rapidly in our knowledge and experience of God and hungry to learn more about spiritual things. I can remember exciting periods in my own Christian journey when I felt I was almost bursting with all the wonderful truths I was learning about God – as a new Christian in my teenage years, as a young mum seeking to draw closer to God and also in midlife as I began to understand more of

the Holy Spirit's work in my life. But we can also experience times when we become discouraged, when we find ourselves disillusioned with other Christians, when the pressures of life cause us to take our eyes off God and stop growing in our faith. If that happens, we may end up going backwards rather than forwards, like my sewing machine – perhaps becoming critical of others, doubting God and even deciding we do not need God at all.

Yes, things happen in life that can draw us into dangerous territory such as this. But whether we feel like it or not, that is precisely when we need to reach out and seek help from those we trust whose faith is real and honest. I am so glad God has always provided me with such people – and I hope you can access that help too.

Whatever our situation in life, however, may we continue to press on, just as Paul chose to do, moving forward rather than slipping backwards, with our eyes on our amazing Lord who will never let us down.

But I focus on this one thing: Forgetting the past and looking forward to what lies ahead, I press on to reach the end of the race and receive the heavenly prize for which God, through Christ Jesus, is calling us.

Philippians 3:13–14, NLT

On Faithfulness and Perseverance

Putting Ourselves Out There

I have a love/hate relationship with a certain, well-known TV show that pits one singer against another. I enjoy hearing the contestants sing but I fear for them as they put themselves in such a vulnerable position, slap-bang in front of a live audience and thousands of viewers, not to mention the judges who will choose between them. I hate to see so many performers head home disappointed, their dream of stardom shattered.

You might not be about to get up and sing, but perhaps you can think of a time when you had to put yourself out there in some capacity and risk being judged. Perhaps you were told to draw or paint a picture at school that was then displayed somewhere. Perhaps you had to play a musical instrument in public. Perhaps you were asked to read aloud something you had written. Can you remember how you felt?

I suspect I relate to these singing contestants so strongly because of my own experiences when younger of playing the piano for scary music examiners and singing in eisteddfods as the judges busily wrote notes about my performance. Yet while these experiences made me feel so vulnerable, they stood me in good stead for playing and singing in various churches in later years – and for standing up and speaking in public as I still often do.

I also believe that, by the grace of God, they have armed me well for my current writing journey. Even now, giving my latest manuscript to others for the first time to critique can be a daunting prospect – and having a new book published can be even more daunting. It has been said that, to be an author, one needs a sensitive heart but the hide of an elephant! Yet if we know God has called and equipped us to write – or paint or sing or play or

dance or create in any way – how important it is to keep putting ourselves out there, whatever others might say or think.

This applies too when speaking about the things of God, whether in a formal setting or informally in our daily lives. In our world today, there are opportunities all around us to share some encouraging word with others and show them God's love. But sometimes it can be hard, can't it? Sometimes, sadly, I still choose to keep quiet and stay in my comfort zone rather than risk being rejected or laughed at or even perhaps verbally abused.

Years ago, when I was about to start studying at theological college and feeling particularly vulnerable doing so in my late forties, a visiting speaker came to our church and, prompted by God, gave me the following verse:

Be on guard. Stand firm in the faith. Be courageous. Be strong.
1 Corinthians 16:13, NLT

Many times, these words kept me going through all the challenges my years at college held, helping me focus on the final goal. Yet surely these words speak to us at every stage of our lives too. So whatever is happening around us right now, may we stand firm, knowing we are secure in God's love. Then in God's strength and with courage, may we each continue to put ourselves out there and endeavour to do all the things God has given us to do.

On Faithfulness and Perseverance

Soldiering On

I sometimes live my life as if those around me will be here forever even if they are not young anymore. Of *course* they will be always there to talk to, I think. Of *course* we can do this or that together. Then the day comes when they are no longer here, and I am shocked. How can this be?

In my more rational moments, I know this is not how things work. Our time on earth is finite, however much we may try to change that. People become ill and cannot be cured. Terrible disasters occur, ending many young lives, while those of us who are left become older and frailer. Yet it can still be hard to accept another's death, whatever age they are. They were here. They were real. They were alive. Now they are no longer with us.

Not long ago, we received news of the deaths of two friends. The first was a gentleman in his nineties who always impressed us with his zest for life and his deep commitment to God and his church. Even until the last year or two, he would bake trays of cakes for youth and outreach events at our church or for the spring fair in the village where he lived. He also loved writing and art and singing – he was an all-round, creative person. Right now, I believe he is rejoicing in heaven in the perfect presence of his Creator God, which is wonderful. Yet it seemed to us as if this larger-than-life person would always be here.

The second was our lovely neighbour, Ruth, who used to live in the unit opposite us until she moved into aged care. She was in her eighties and had been unwell for some years, yet each day when she could, she would sit on her little stool in the garden, digging away and caring for each plant and flower. She was a writer too – such an intelligent, interesting person.

On Faithfulness and Perseverance

But above all, she loved God wholeheartedly and served in the Salvation Army all her life. We were still in the process of moving into our unit when she told me she had been praying for us for some time. On occasions too, she would come to our door, holding some beans or tomatoes or other produce from her garden, and tell me they were the 'first-fruits' from her harvest and a gift to us. It is wonderful to think that, right now, she is also completely whole again in God's presence. She was a faithful soldier all her life – and has now marched right on into heaven.

This news of the passing of these two faithful followers of Jesus has made me look at my own life again. There is no doubt both loved God with all their hearts. They served God and others their whole lives and were indeed ready to meet their Lord. In my mind, I can hear each one of them saying, along with the Apostle Paul, not in any boasting way but as a simple statement of fact:

I have fought the good fight, I have finished the race, I have kept the faith.
2 Timothy 4:7

May you and I be able to declare this too, with true humility but also deep certainty when we reach our own journey's end.

On Faithfulness and Perseverance

When the Pieces Fit

I am definitely not a seasoned solver of jigsaw puzzles. I enjoyed helping my husband a while ago with two puzzles I gave him as birthday presents – maybe even when he did not happen to want or need my help! But the one-thousand-piece puzzle he gave me in return managed to exact any revenge he wished to exact and then some.

Eventually, after much concentrated effort, I conquered the challenge. But then I saw one extra puzzle piece lying on the table nearby. I had noticed it on and off while working on the jigsaw and wondered where it could possibly fit. It did not look quite the same as the other pieces so, each time, I put it aside. Now there it still was, with no more spaces available where it could go.

For a while, I gazed at it in disbelief. Surely a jigsaw puzzle company would not make that sort of mistake? I checked the completed puzzle again – nope, definitely no spare spots anywhere. Then my mind jumped to the possibility that, somewhere out there, some other poor person might well be trying to complete their own puzzle, only to discover one crucial piece missing. I would hate that to happen to me, after all my efforts. Someone then suggested the manufacturers might have included an extra piece just to make their puzzles harder and tease their poor victims. But again, surely not. Or . . . could they?

Not long after, I packed my completed puzzle away, spare piece and all. Maybe sometime in the future, I will do it again, forgetting about that pesky extra piece. But there is one thing I experienced as I worked on my puzzle that I will never forget. A few times, I tried to add a piece that *seemed*

right but did not make the satisfying, little click that would tell me it fitted perfectly in that spot. Yet whenever I did hear that click, it immediately brought back a memory from around sixty years ago.

In 1963, a friend invited me to a camp for high-school students run by her church denomination. One night after the speaker had invited us to come forward and commit our lives to Christ, I was among the first to do so. I was overwhelmed by the amazing thought that God knew *me* and loved *me*, that I *mattered* to God. Suddenly, the fact that Jesus Christ loved me and died for me made sense. It was as if a veil lifted from my eyes in an instant and I knew I had found the reason I was on this earth – to love and serve God forever. In that moment too, something deep inside me seemed to fall into place with a satisfying 'click' like the sound of the last piece of a child's wooden jigsaw puzzle dropping into place.

One day, we will see the entire, completed picture of our lives from God's perspective. One day, we will understand fully. But for now, may we keep on trusting in the One who loves us totally and fits all the pieces of our lives together in the best way possible.

Now we see things imperfectly, like puzzling reflections in a mirror, but then we will see everything with perfect clarity.

1 Corinthians 13:12, NLT

On Faithfulness and Perseverance

Being Prepared

When I was a Girl Guide in my early teens, we enjoyed many interesting activities, both indoor and outdoor. We also regularly went on hikes and camps, but one thing remained constant whatever we did. We always wore our Guide uniform, a navy-blue dress with four large pockets. In those pockets, we carried all sorts of things that might come in handy out in the bush, including a compass, a notebook and pencil, some Band-Aids, a plastic groundsheet and even a snakebite kit back then. Also, the light-blue tie we wore, always folded in a specific way, was in fact a triangular piece of material that could double as an arm sling if needs be. Our Girl Guide motto was 'Be prepared' – and we certainly took that to heart.

This motto came to mind again recently as I read in Nehemiah 4 how, halfway through rebuilding the walls of Jerusalem, the Jews became discouraged and afraid when they discovered that their enemies planned to attack. However, Nehemiah and the other leaders prayed (verse 9), then stationed the people in strategic positions with swords, spears and bows ready and urged them to stand firm: 'Don't be afraid of the enemy! Remember the LORD, who is great and glorious' (Nehemiah 4:14b, NLT).

With God's help, the enemy's plot was foiled, but Nehemiah remained vigilant. He organised half the men to protect the people, while the other half kept labouring to finish the wall. He also ordered the builders to work with their swords strapped on, ready to fight at a moment's notice, and the labourers to carry all their building materials in one hand and a weapon in the other (verses 17–18). But that was not all. Because the workers were scattered, he organised a man to sound the trumpet to warn everyone,

On Faithfulness and Perseverance

should the enemy attack (verses 19–20). Yes, Nehemiah was determined to be prepared and made sure his people were too.

As I pictured all this military activity in my mind, I realised what a powerful image it is for my life today. I may not have human invaders on all sides, plotting to bring me down. Yet I am well aware of the extremely alert, cunning enemy Paul warns us about who constantly seeks to discourage, especially when I set out to tackle something I believe God particularly wants me to do:

For we are not fighting against flesh-and-blood enemies, but against evil rulers and authorities of the unseen world, against mighty powers in this dark world, and against evil spirits in the heavenly places.

Ephesians 6:12, NLT

I cannot speak for you, but, unlike Nehemiah's men, I need both hands to work on my writing each day. Yet I can still put on the armour Paul goes on to urge the Ephesians – and us – to wear, including the sword of the Spirit, the word of God (Ephesians 6:13–17). I can also pray constantly, just as Nehemiah did and as Paul taught too (Ephesians 6:18). Even as I keep working, I can hold these amazing weapons from God in my hands, so to speak, stay alert and, just as Nehemiah did, keep trusting in our great and glorious God rather than give in to fear.

May you too always be found fully armed and prepared as you seek to serve God each day.

On Faithfulness and Perseverance

Taking Courage

One night, I received a phone call from a distraught friend.

'I'm in a terrible pickle!' she gasped. 'We filled in a form on my computer with all my details and now I've been scammed. Please pray!'

The next morning, I received a text from another friend. She had been unwell and was facing a scary doctor's appointment.

'I would appreciate prayer,' she said. 'I don't want to cough in the middle of my eye injection.'

My heart went out to these friends who both needed God's protection – and the courage to keep trusting God in their daunting situations.

I began to pray for them, yet I soon became almost overwhelmed with fear myself and doubtful that God could rescue them. Then I realised I was falling for one of those old traps the enemy loves to set for us. I could almost hear him sniggering at my lack of faith and, at that point, became determined not to let him win – over me or my friends. So I prayed again, entrusting them to our loving, all-powerful Lord.

We all need courage to face life's challenges and stand firm in our faith, resist the enemy and remain prayerful. Recently, I started reading Acts again. I marvelled at the change in the disciples – and Peter in particular – when the Holy Spirit comes upon them at Pentecost (Acts 2). Immediately after, Peter does not hesitate to address the crowd who have gathered and call them to repentance (Acts 2:38). After the lame man at the temple gates is healed, Peter boldly preaches to all those present in the temple courtyard

(Acts 3). Then, when he and John are jailed and hauled before the rulers, elders and teachers of the law, he again does not hold back: 'It is by the name of Jesus Christ of Nazareth, whom you crucified but whom God raised from the dead, that this man stands before you healed' (Acts 4:10b).

I find the religious leaders' baffled response so interesting too: 'When they saw the courage of Peter and John and realised that they were unschooled, ordinary men, they were astonished and they took note that these men had been with Jesus' (Acts 4:13).

But this is not the end. After Peter and John are commanded not to speak or teach in Jesus' name again, they declare they simply *have* to (Acts 4:20). They are threatened further but finally released – at which point they head back to the other believers. Then a wonderful time of prayer ensues, during which the Holy Spirit fills everyone present: 'After they prayed, the place where they were meeting was shaken. And they were all filled with the Holy Spirit and spoke the word of God boldly' (Acts 4:31).

Peter and the apostles then continue to proclaim the good news of Jesus day after day with amazing courage and faithfulness (Acts 5:12–42).

I want to face life with more of this same courage and boldness, don't you? Although we cannot spend time with Jesus in human form as Peter and John did, we can still talk with him and learn from him each day. Also, like those early believers, we have God's Spirit within us who will fill and empower us to face whatever comes our way. So may we too, like them, trust God, step out boldly and give it our all.

On Faithfulness and Perseverance

Between His Shoulders

I love it when I discover some new pearl of wisdom in something I am reading, some truth that really resonates and makes me sit up and take notice. I keep a journal where I jot down such things – and what a feast of wisdom and insight it can be when I look back after several months and read them all in one go. As I glance through these entries, I find, first and foremost, many quotes from different parts of Scripture that have encouraged, challenged or reassured me in some way. But I may also find excerpts from thoughtful, contemplative works such as those by Frederick Buechner, Annie Dillard and Thomas Merton; from the insightful poetry of T.S. Eliot and Mary Oliver; from non-fiction books about creativity such as *The Soul Tells a Story* by Vinita Hampton Wright and *Bird by Bird* by Anne Lamott; and from the various novels I read from time to time too.

One would think that, after all these years, I would have noted down every Scripture verse that could possibly encourage, challenge or reassure me. Yet God never ceases to surprise me with little gems that jump out at me, even if I have read these same sections many times over.

This happened again not long ago when I was reading Deuteronomy 33, the account of how Moses blesses the Israelite tribes before his impending death. In verse 12, he says the following to the tribe of Benjamin:

Let the beloved of the LORD rest secure in him,
for he shields him all day long,
and the one the LORD loves rests between his shoulders.

Deuteronomy 33:12

On Rest and Peace

These words conjure up some wonderful imagery in my mind. Do they do the same for you? It seems, from what I could discover, that this verse might refer to the way shepherds from time to time used to carry an injured or perhaps favourite lamb slung across their shoulders. But the picture that came to my mind as I read these words was of a strong, tall warrior using his body to shield someone a lot smaller and weaker from the advancing enemy. The intended victim was clinging on tightly behind, arms around the rescuer's waist, head turned to the side and pressed firmly into the spot between the rescuer's shoulder blades. No one could touch him (or her) while this strong, courageous defender stood firm and continued to act as a human shield, ready to risk all to protect the one holding on so tightly.

For me, this image also resonated with the following well-known words:

You are my hiding-place;
   you will protect me from trouble
   and surround me with songs of deliverance.

Psalm 32:7

What a privilege to enjoy the comfort and security of such a precious hiding-place, protected and at rest between the Lord's shoulders! I might be in the middle of a battle but I can be at peace as I lean against him. Because I am his beloved child, I know he will never grow tired of being my shield and protector but will stand firm to the end and bring me safely home at last to be with him forever.

May you know that same deep peace and security as you too rest your head between the shoulders of our loving Lord.

On Rest and Peace

Watching Weeds Rejoice

At our old house, we had a large backyard spread over two levels. I love gardening but rarely had time for it. On the other hand, my husband hates it. I grew up with a father who was an avid gardener so I was able to learn much from him as I watched him work. However, my husband did not have this opportunity in his family. As a result, while he was prepared to mow lawns and remove garden waste, he often had great difficulty telling a weed from a 'real plant'.

So . . . what to do? We could have decided to put more time and effort into gardening, or perhaps even paid someone to help out. Alternately, we could have let the weeds hold sway – although looking at a messy garden every day would have been quite a challenge for me. Then, one day, I discovered a completely different perspective on gardening – or weeding in particular – during a phone conversation with my dear friend in the Blue Mountains west of Sydney. At the time, she had a very large garden but she was almost eighty years old and found it impossible to look after it all. Yet she seemed far from depressed as she described its messy state to me.

'Oh, I'm having a *wonderful* time watching all my weeds rejoice! They're so happy that no one's bothering them. The vegetables have gone to seed too but that's good – we can use the seed another season. Anyway, it's all so colourful – and there's always something to look at.'

Watching all the weeds rejoice. What a novel thought!

It surely is a matter of perspective, isn't it? My friend could not do much about her weeds so she chose to accept them. She was determined not to

let them rob her of the enjoyment of her garden and even saw in them a unique kind of beauty, with each one relishing the warmer spring weather, breathing in the clean, mountain air and almost defiantly rejoicing over their moment in the sun while not being interfered with in any way. My friend displayed more than a little sense of humour in the midst of her situation too – again such a vital ingredient for moving through life in a calm, unruffled way. She was at peace with herself, with God and with the world, including nature.

What a wonderful attitude to have in life. We can choose to dwell on the negatives of a particular situation or focus instead on the positives – and we can also choose to see God at work even in the 'weeds' we encounter in our lives. To me, my friend's acceptance of her situation seemed to reflect something at least of the attitude the Apostle Paul had learnt to have in his life:

I have learned to be content whatever the circumstances. I know what it is to be in need, and I know what it is to have plenty. I have learned the secret of being content in any and every situation, whether well fed or hungry, whether living in plenty or in want.

Philippians 4:11b–13

I hope I can soon cultivate the same attitude and be much more content and at peace, whatever shape the 'weeds' might take in my life – and I hope you can too.

On Rest and Peace

The Voice of Peace

One day as I sat reading my Bible, I found myself suddenly swept back into the distant past. In a trice, I was a young girl again, watching my father struggle to his feet and declare in a resigned voice, 'Well, I'd better get back to the gardening. No rest for the wicked.' In my mind, I could even picture every detail of his appearance – dark-blue singlet under an open, checked shirt, khaki shorts and worn, old boots. You see, I had just read the words of Isaiah 57:21: '"There is no peace," says my God, "for the wicked."'

To me, the message my father always seemed to take from this verse was that he needed to keep working hard in life, perhaps as a way of getting right with God. At that time, however, he claimed to have rejected the idea of eternal life in any form and used to tell us with finality, 'When you're dead, you're dead.'

I was unable to see him in the last weeks of his life but, thankfully, it seems he may have changed his mind about such things. I hope he did – I like to think of him at rest and peace with God, which is what God is talking about in the following verse from Isaiah:

> **For this is what the high and exalted One says –**
> **he who lives for ever, whose name is holy:**
> **'I live in a high and holy place,**
> **but also with the one who is contrite and lowly in spirit,**
> **to revive the spirit of the lowly**
> **and to revive the heart of the contrite . . .**

Isaiah 57:15

On Rest and Peace

Verse 19 adds:

> Peace, peace, to those far and near,'
>   says the Lord. 'And I will heal them.

Isaiah 57:19

We all need God's peace in a world where so many competing voices try to bring us down and make us feel anxious, frustrated or inadequate. Yes, there will hopefully be many things in life that give us great peace and joy too – a loving family, good friends, an interesting job, a comfortable home, success in some area. But God's peace goes far beyond all of these.

I have always loved Jesus' words to his disciples before his crucifixion, warning them about what lay ahead. I like to imagine the sound of his voice as he spoke to them – a voice filled with authority but also with love:

Peace I leave with you; my peace I give you. I do not give to you as the world gives. Do not let your hearts be troubled and do not be afraid.

John 14:27

Jesus' peace is different from anything the world offers. It is far deeper and more profound. It is eternal. It is not merely the absence of trouble but rather the presence of the Prince of Peace within us in the person of his Holy Spirit, strengthening us and whispering words of comfort to us.

May God enable us to close our ears to those voices that discourage and confuse us or offer a peace that does not truly satisfy. Instead, may God enable us to choose to be among those who are 'contrite and lowly in spirit', who listen for God's loving voice and hear it as clearly as I heard my own earthly father's voice that day in my imagination.

On Rest and Peace

Pure Joy

I love waiting at the airport to welcome people. As I do, I often like to guess why others around me are there too. Are they possibly meeting a parent, grandparent, son or daughter – or perhaps a precious partner? Some look hopefully at the exit door every few seconds. Some have children or whole families with them who are all restless with excitement. Others try to act more nonchalantly, yet their nervous mannerisms speak volumes.

'There she is!' we hear at last – and soon there is a rush towards some traveller whose face is transformed with joy at the sight of loved ones.

It is a delight to watch these moments of unadulterated joy, isn't it? I have seen them in other contexts too – and I could never forget one such instance that caught me completely by surprise.

I was holding our 6-week-old granddaughter and talking softly to her. As I did, I noticed how her eyes seemed fixed on some spot beyond my head. I turned away for a moment – and when I looked back at her, she was gazing straight at me with the widest, most delightful smile on her cute, little face. No, it was not merely a grimace from some troublesome wind. It was one of those first, truly social smiles that are so precious and special.

I could not take my eyes off her. Her smile transformed her whole face. I noticed too how her eyes shone with a deep, inner radiance. It was as if she was saying in the only way she could, 'Hello! I'm here – and I think I'd like to connect with you.' It was as if some innate sense of joy had suddenly bubbled up inside her – as if her little spirit was reaching out for recognition

On Rest and Peace

and for some sort of warm, loving welcome to this world. Needless to say, this grandmother was utterly besotted.

Yet this experience also challenged me. Years earlier, in a very busy period of my life, a Christian friend told me he could not see much joy in me at that point. I know we all go through sad, difficult times in our lives, but I had no real excuse. I was merely 'worried and upset about many things', as Martha was when Jesus visited her home (Luke 10:41). I had almost forgotten what it was like to allow God's Spirit to fill me with the amazing peace and joy I knew was available to me.

Soon after, I copied out a blunt question the Apostle Paul asked some believers at one stage from the old Bible I used then and placed it above my desk: 'What has happened to all your joy?' (Galatians 4:15a, NIV 1984). I truly wanted God's joy to radiate from me and reflect God's heart to others, so this question served as a good reminder to rejoice and rest in God's love once again.

At times today, I still need such reminders, and perhaps you do too. May we learn to look to God for the refreshment we need and experience again the deep joy and peace found in God alone.

But let all who take refuge in you be glad;
    let them ever sing for joy.
Spread your protection over them,
    that those who love your name may rejoice in you.

Psalm 5:11

On Rest and Peace

Inhabiting the Moment

It is a well-known fact in our family that I dislike food shopping. It seems such a waste of time to me to trail around the supermarket, trying to think of something as mundane as what meals to cook when I could be at my desk writing.

One day, I was heading home from shopping, feeling frustrated I had again wasted so much time, when my whole perspective changed. As I drove down our street, I saw an amazing, heart-warming sight. Evenly spaced across the road in a little line were a mother and father duck and eight striped ducklings! They were heading straight for the park opposite and, no doubt, down the slope into the nearby creek from there. I slowed down, hoping they would perhaps return to the safety of the footpath, but they kept waddling on as if they owned the entire road. With little alternative, I stopped the car and sat gaping at them in disbelief. There was nothing I could do but take in the moment and, as I admired the serene, unhurried way they went about their business, I found myself relaxing and grinning.

Then I noticed two real-estate agents, a man and a woman, walking along the nearby footpath and canvassing for potential sales. They seemed harassed and preoccupied, but I eventually managed to attract the woman's attention at least. I smiled at her and pointed towards the spot where the ducks were crossing the road, a sight she had apparently missed altogether. She did not return my smile, however, and gave the ducks only a cursory glance before moving on.

I immediately felt sorry for her. What a lovely experience she had missed out on.

On Rest and Peace

At that point, I went to take a photo but realised that was probably not a good thing to do while sitting in my car in the middle of our normally busy road. By then, the ducks had almost made it across and soon disappeared into the park. I quickly drove on and turned into our yard, then raced back to take my photo, but was too late. All I could see of my duck family was an occasional little head bobbing above the long grass, then the rear ends of the mother and father duck as they disappeared into the creek.

Much later, I was still smiling at the beautiful, little event I had witnessed. Then I began to wonder if it had been sent directly to me from God. It was as if God was saying, 'Oh Jo-Anne, here you are, so preoccupied with all sorts of worries and frustrations and so wishing you were doing something else that you are almost oblivious of the beautiful moments right in front of your nose. How about you do life *my* way and at *my* pace for a change?' I had thought those real-estate agents were missing out on something lovely, yet I too needed to realise how unwilling I was to treasure and live fully in the present moment with God and be at peace as I went about my daily tasks.

May we all learn to be still and experience God much more in the small, mundane moments in life, as well as in the big, exciting ones.

Be still, and know that I am God.

Psalm 46:10a

On Rest and Peace

Finding That Quiet Place

'Which way should I head today?' I ask myself as I leave our house one morning for my regular walk. 'I could set out down our street, under the busy main road, past various businesses, then left along a section of bike path to the next street and home again – quite a short round trip. I could veer right instead on that bike path, under the railway line, along the edge of the river, through the beautiful grounds of the nearby university, then home again. Or I could go up the hill towards our local school and shops. Which one should I choose today?'

Feeling a little restless, I decide to try somewhere different. I drive down to the ferry wharf and park my car under a shady tree. There before me, the lovely, flat bike path winds its way east beside the river towards the bridge and beyond. I set off, walking fast. For some reason, I sense I have not so much chosen this route today as it has chosen me. Could the fact that I am speaking from Psalm 23 later in the week have subconsciously influenced my choice? After all, the psalm does talk about being led beside quiet waters.

The Lord is my shepherd, I lack nothing.
He makes me lie down in green pastures,
he leads me beside quiet waters,
he refreshes my soul.

Psalm 23:1–3a

The path curves around past a children's playground and a grove of tall eucalypts. I am tempted to stop and sit on a seat there in the shade but press on. Cyclists overtake me and smile as do one or two other walkers. Soon, I begin to hear the whoosh of traffic and realise I have almost

reached the bridge. I pass beneath it, then notice on my left a number of enormous, new apartment blocks in various stages of completion. Some seem occupied already, while others still have scaffolding around them. I can hear workmen shouting to one another on these sites and the noise of power tools and other building equipment.

I then discover a brand new, shaded, picnic-table area nearby, right beside the river, and decide to rest there for a while. As I do, I realise I can hear loud noises coming from either side of me. On my left, there are those workmen on the building site, drilling, hammering and calling out. On my right, there is the constant hum of traffic as it makes its way over the bridge. Yet, in between, right where I am, is this wonderful, peaceful spot beside the deep, quietly flowing river. Even as I sit there, gazing at the water, I see three pelicans land – oh so gracefully – on its surface and float along as if they own the entire river, unperturbed by the noise around them.

In that instant, I sense God saying to me, 'See, even in the midst of the hustle and bustle of your life when things are happening all around you and press in on you, I can provide those quiet waters that will restore you deep in your spirit. Stay close to me. Keep listening to me.'

I relax on the outside and the inside. I am held close in my quiet place with God – and I am so grateful.

On Rest and Peace

Just Joey

Can you remember a time when you saw something on display somewhere and felt you simply *had* to buy it? This happened to me not long after we moved into our beautiful, new unit. At the time, I was strolling around a plant nursery, trying to decide which roses to buy for the small garden beside our balcony. The previous owner had grown several roses there, but once he was no longer able to care for them, the gardeners had removed them. Despite their efforts, however, one single rose bush had defied all odds and come back to life so, in order to balance our garden out a little, I asked if I could plant a couple more. Yet I did not know which rose to choose out of the many on offer.

Finally, I decided on a deep-red rose, 'Mr Lincoln'. Its blooms were not quite the shape I wanted but they had a beautiful, strong perfume and the plant seemed vigorous and hardy. Then a label on a pretty, apricot-coloured rose nearby caught my eye – 'Just Joey'. Now how could I resist? After all, my name is Jo-Anne – but the name my family often called me when I was growing up was Joey. Surely I *had* to have that 'Just Joey' rose in my garden as we began this new phase of our lives?

Yet there was another reason the name of this rose had caught my eye. For a long time, I had kept the outline of a memoir on my computer, waiting until I felt the moment was right for me to explore it further. Eventually, I did – and gradually, this outline grew and developed into my second non-fiction book, *Becoming Me*. But can you guess my original idea for its title? Yes indeed – *Just Joey*.

On Rest and Peace

Apparently, my rose, 'Just Joey', was named after the wife of the head of a nursery company in the UK. But to me, these two little words seem to sum up my life as I have learnt and grown and made mistakes and grown some more and stepped out to become more of the person I believe God created me to be. God knew all about me before I was born and created me as a unique human being with my own particular personality and gifts:

For you created my inmost being;
you knit me together in my mother's womb.
I praise you because I am fearfully and wonderfully made.

Psalm 139:13–14a

God knew every twist and turn in my journey too and has been with me all the way, even when certain strong winds in my life threatened to snap my fragile stem, as occasionally happens to my new rosebush. Today, I feel so blessed to be 'Just Joey', to rest in who I am in God, to be less afraid of being all I was created to be and less jealous of those with different gifts and abilities who seem to have achieved more in life than I have.

My 'Just Joey' rose is unique, with its delicate, frilled petals and gentle perfume – and you and I are unique too, just as God created us to be. May we rest in that truth each day, be at peace with who we are and so thankful for all God has given us.

On Rest and Peace

Packing Our Bags

I watched my neighbour's eyes fill with tears as she told me about her great-grandson. His grandfather had recently passed away and, in order to explain this sad event to him, his family told him his grandfather had gone to 'the sky'.

'I want to go and see him,' this little boy replied.

'We can't do that,' they told him.

'Well, you get him to come here.'

'We can't do that either.'

Because this little boy's parents have separated, he is used to packing his bag and staying with one parent for a week, then with the other the following week. So he decided to get his bag, head for the front door and try to find his grandfather in the sky himself.

While reflecting on the image of this little boy looking and hoping, I remembered some strong words Paul wrote, warning Timothy about those for whom godliness was only a means to financial gain:

But godliness with contentment is great gain. For we brought nothing into the world, and we can take nothing out of it.

1 Timothy 6:6–7

My neighbour's great-grandson sadly cannot take his little bag with him to visit his grandfather or now see him at all – and neither can we take anything with us when we leave this world. Surely then, Paul's words are an important reminder to us to think about the things we focus on pursuing and accumulating in life.

On Rest and Peace

Then one day, a lady at church told us about something that happened to her husband and her while overseas. They were in Rome and had to wait some hours until their B&B accommodation was available. They parked their hire car at a shopping centre and looked around for a while but, when they returned to their car, it had been broken into and everything they owned stolen. All they had left were the clothes they were wearing and whatever else they had with them.

That evening, the B&B owner contacted the police for them to try to get their property back, but to no avail. Yet our church friend was calm through it all because, just that morning, she felt God had told her that, whatever happened that day, he would be watching over her.

In fact, she was so calm that the B&B owner became quite puzzled. 'You seem kind of "zen-like",' he told her – at which point she explained what she felt God had said to her.

Eventually, this lady and her husband continued their trip, with only one much smaller bag each. As she told us this, she commented how free it felt to travel so much lighter.

This story caused me to reflect even further on the baggage I myself am carrying right now through this world. Is it light? Is it something I can let go of without too many pangs? More importantly, am I putting my time and energy into those things that really matter, such as those Paul goes on to mention to Timothy: 'But you, man of God, flee from all this, and pursue righteousness, godliness, faith, love, endurance and gentleness' (1 Timothy 6:11)?

May our bags be packed full to overflowing with righteousness, godliness, faith, love, endurance and gentleness too, when our time comes to meet God face to face.

On Rest and Peace

Making Music Together

In recent times, I have embarked on yet another new vocation. I have become our 9-year-old granddaughter's piano teacher. This is something I would not normally aspire to do but, given the cost of piano lessons and the difficulty of accessing them easily, we decided this was the best option. Picture me then, seated with Maxine on my right at the piano as we navigate our way through John Thompson's *Easiest Piano Course* – an interesting journey indeed.

Maxine is very musical. Prior to this, she has played little pieces from memory and by ear, without being able to read music. But now we have well and truly embarked on the adventure of knowing what all those funny notes are called and where and how to play them on the piano, not to mention the names and meanings of various other musical symbols. I never want to spoil her enjoyment of music by being too pedantic and exacting so, each lesson, we try to have fun together as well. A large part of our fun happens when I manage to play the accompaniment provided alongside most of the little pieces she learns while she perseveres with her part.

In the process of teaching our granddaughter, I have learnt a few things myself, not least of which is how to be more patient with a bubbly, little girl who cannot seem to keep still beside me and whose attention can tend to wander, even though she is keen to learn. But then, often when I am about to give up and decide we have had enough for one lesson, she shows me she has indeed understood all the new concepts I have taught her and can play every note correctly.

On Rest and Peace

I have learnt to be patient too when Maxine wants to go back and play her favourite piece time and time again. This piece has a particularly mellow, tuneful accompaniment and I applaud her musical ear and taste, so I usually acquiesce. But I draw the line at joining her in playing 'Chopsticks', which she delights in choosing just to tease me!

As I have gained more patience in teaching Maxine, I believe I have also learnt something more about God. Surely at times, from God's perspective, I must seem unfocused in my Christian journey and so inattentive to what God is showing me as I give in to distractions and flip this way and that. Surely at other times, I must seem content to stay put or revert to old, familiar patterns of behaviour rather than forge on and learn new rhythms and melodies in my life. Surely too, God has been so much more patient and understanding with me than I will ever be with Maxine. But just as occurs in our piano lessons, I know there are also moments when I glimpse more of God, when I do hear and understand those lessons God is teaching me, and when God and I enjoy playing beautiful music together.

May there be many more priceless moments like these, not only in Maxine's piano lessons, but in my life and yours in general as we journey on with God.

Take my yoke upon you and learn from me, for I am gentle and humble in heart, and you will find rest for your souls.

Matthew 11:29

On Rest and Peace

Remembering the Basics

It is strange how easily we can forget those simple strategies that help us so much in life, isn't it? We may decide that some sort of daily exercise benefits our health but, before long, we let this practice slip. We may realise that working at a computer too long after dinner can rob us of a good night's sleep, yet I still decide to do this often. Time and time again, we can so easily push to one side those wise, practical ways we know are right and, instead, choose a path we may later regret.

I was reminded of this recently when I visited a physio for some help with managing my sore shoulders better. He questioned me about my posture as I sit and type at my desk, often for hours each day, and I soon realised that, while I had remembered some basic things to watch, I had clearly forgotten others. Yes, I have a good desk chair, I told him. Yes, I sit close to my keyboard so that I can type with my elbows touching my body and with my computer screen at eye level. But no, I often sit with my legs crossed instead of keeping my feet flat on the floor. Also, my husband has told me many times that I sit hunched over at my computer, with my neck craned forward as I peer at the screen.

In one way, I was relieved my shoulder issues were not due merely to old age. But in another, I was annoyed I had fallen into such silly habits. It can be a bitter pill to swallow when we have no one but ourselves to blame for the things that happen to us. Now, each time I sit down at my desk, I try to remember to check my posture, then regularly square my shoulders and roll them around to get rid of any tension. Also, three times a day, I do some basic exercises my physio recommended.

On Rest and Peace

All this has caused me to reflect on other parts of my life too where I am prone to forget the basics. How easy I find it each day to see the emails on my computer waiting to be answered or those posts or blogs waiting to be written and launch into tackling them straight away, without stopping to reflect with God on the day ahead. How easy it can be for me to fall into old habits of worrying about things rather than praying and trusting God with them. How easy it can be for all of us, it seems to me, to forget we are God's much-loved children, so that we feel we are alone in our battles, lean on our own strength and forge ahead as if everything is up to us.

Instead, before we step into our days, may we stop, remember the basics of who we are in God and consciously rest safe and secure in our loving Father's arms once again.

He came to that which was his own, but his own did not receive him. Yet to all who did receive him, to those who believed in his name, he gave the right to become children of God.

John 1:11–12

The Spirit himself testifies with our spirit that we are God's children.

Romans 8:16

On Rest and Peace

Coming First

I had made my way bright and early to a large shopping centre nearby. There were two things I needed and I was definitely focused on finding these, then scuttling back home. But as I passed a clothing store selling 'intimate apparel', I stopped and gasped out loud. It was not the very skimpy garments that caught my eye. Instead, it was the bold sign written in large letters featured prominently in the window – 'I COME FIRST'.

Really?

Despite my slightly shocked state, I realised it was merely a marketing slogan, an overstatement aimed at persuading potential customers that they deserve to pamper themselves and buy that expensive, perhaps frivolous item, rather than a cheaper, more practical item or something for someone other than themselves. Maybe there are times when we *should* do such things. Some of us may well need to learn to care for ourselves better and put ourselves first more often so that we can regain our health and strength. But . . . should we come first *all* the time? Is that how we are supposed to live our lives? Is that what God wants us to do?

I also remembered a TV ad I had seen that week for a reality series that apparently 'everyone is waiting to see', according to its promoters. I had gasped when I heard one contestant declare something to the effect that she likes to make all the decisions because 'it always has to be my way'! Imagine living or even being friends with someone with such a selfish, arrogant attitude where everything has to suit them and where their needs always come before the needs of others.

On Christlikeness

I think God calls us to march to the beat of a different drum, don't you? In the middle of the shopping centre that morning, I thought of the parable Jesus told when he went to eat at the home of a prominent Pharisee and noticed how the guests chose the places of honour at the table (Luke 14). In this parable, Jesus urges those present to take the lowest place and leave it to the host to invite them to move up higher. Then Jesus ends with the following: 'For those who exalt themselves will be humbled, and those who humble themselves will be exalted' (Luke 14:11, NLT).

Some challenging words the Apostle Paul wrote about putting others' welfare before our own also came to mind:

Don't be selfish; don't try to impress others. Be humble, thinking of others as better than yourselves. Don't look out only for your own interests, but take an interest in others, too.

Philippians 2:3–4, NLT

Paul goes on to urge us to remember Jesus, who put everything aside for us, became a man and humbled himself completely, even to the point of dying on a cross:

You must have the same attitude that Christ Jesus had. Though he was God . . . he gave up his divine privileges; he took the humble position of a slave.

Philippians 2:5–7a, NLT

What a different attitude from the one that declares, 'I come first.' This can be a challenge to take on board today, but may we embrace it anyway, however hard it might be. May we remember Jesus' example and dare to be different, putting others first, just as he did.

On Christlikeness

The Battles We Fight

It can be easy to judge others, can't it? As I watch the news each evening, I often do just that when I hear of someone who has reportedly committed a crime or some celebrity who has gone off the rails. Admittedly, their track record might speak for itself, but we do not know all the facts. So often, we make up our minds about people on a very small amount of information that may, after all, be quite biased.

I remember some students I once taught at an exclusive girls' school when I was all of 21 years old. In my naivety, I assumed there was no excuse for any of them to do poorly or behave badly. After all, most came from privileged backgrounds. Yet I recall one boarder who had trouble passing any exam and would rarely speak in class. When she did, she was quite aggressive. What internal battles was she fighting? Homesickness? Loneliness? Lack of self-esteem? I never did enquire further and ignored her, failing her in an exam by only one mark when, in grace, I could have encouraged her and found that mark somewhere.

Twenty years later, I returned to teaching, ending up at a school where classes were graded. I taught Introductory Language to all ten Year Seven classes there. Can you imagine how keen my poor tenth class was to learn a foreign language? I worked hard to make my lessons interesting and accessible for them. I cajoled. I threatened. I yelled a lot – and, in my heart, I judged them as hopeless. Only occasionally did I ever wonder what difficulties they might be facing in their home and family life. Instead, I ranted and raved when homework was not done or the relevant workbook was not brought to class.

On Christlikeness

Recently, I read some words attributed to the Jewish philosopher, Philo of Alexandria: 'Be kind to all, because everyone is fighting a great battle.' Those students in my classes were no doubt fighting lots of battles, just as many around me today doubtless are too, in some shape or form. I know about some of these in the lives of relatives and friends. But what other struggles lie behind the faces of those in our street, in our unit blocks, at the shopping centre, on the train or bus, at work – at church?

Appearances can be deceptive. Someone may seem to have it all together but, inside, they may well be fighting ongoing emotional battles or wrestling with huge spiritual issues. Some might agonise over things we feel are relatively trivial – but they are real to them. Some might gain a quick victory in a particular battle, while others may struggle a lifetime. Who am I to judge them?

Jesus spoke some strong words about this on one occasion:

Do not judge, and you will not be judged. Do not condemn, and you will not be condemned. Forgive, and you will be forgiven. Give, and it will be given to you. A good measure, pressed down, shaken together and running over, will be poured into your lap. For with the measure you use, it will be measured to you.
Luke 6:37–8

May you and I take good note of these words and endeavour each day to be much more sensitive to others' struggles.

On Christlikeness

The Fine Art of Imitation

Our youngest granddaughter and I were blowing bubbles together outside one day when she announced she wanted to dance for me. She was only four and had never been to ballet classes, but that did not deter her at all. With a distinctly professional air, she slowly moved her arms around her head, then caressed her face with her hands and gazed up at me with such a soulful expression that I was hard-pressed not to laugh. Some further interesting movements followed, until her carefully executed performance ended with a flourish and a most creditable version of the splits.

I was amazed. How on earth had she learnt to dance so expressively? It could only have been through watching movies like *Frozen* or *Moana* or *Cinderella* or perhaps something else on YouTube. All she knows, she has learnt by imitating the heroines in her favourite shows – even down to their dreamy facial expressions.

Later, back at our unit, she decided to play our piano but then stopped abruptly. 'Wait – I need to find some music,' she declared.

She proceeded to drag an old music album out of our piano stool, open it and place it carefully in front of her exactly how she must have seen 'real' pianists do. Then, with one hand tracing the notes on the page, she proceeded to play gently with the other, checking often to ensure she was 'reading' the music correctly.

Again, I struggled not to laugh. At that age, she had no idea what all the funny-shaped notes and symbols meant on those pages but was determined to act as if she did.

On Christlikeness

As I thought more about our ability to imitate, I realised there may be some negative aspects to it at times. If a piece of jewellery contains synthetic diamonds, it is considered much less valuable – perhaps even a fake. If a singer sounds too much like the original artist who made a song famous, they can be criticised and written off as unoriginal. At times, someone may deliberately decide to imitate another person's voice or mannerisms in public in order to ridicule or put them down. Young children, who learn either consciously or unconsciously by imitating adults and older siblings, can all too often pick up certain undesirable attitudes and behaviour we carelessly exhibit.

Yet copying others can also be a positive, worthwhile endeavour. How wonderful it is when we notice children beginning to act in respectful and responsible ways that they have gleaned from imitating their parents' positive example. But how much more it must delight God when we set our hearts and minds to imitating Jesus, just as the Apostle Paul sought to do. In 1 Corinthians 4:16, he urges the early believers to imitate him, Paul, which I used to think was surely an arrogant thing to write. Yet a few chapters later, we realise Paul can legitimately do this because he himself seeks to follow Jesus with his whole heart:

Follow my example, as I follow the example of Christ.

1 Corinthians 11:1

One day, I would love to be able to write the same words as confidently as Paul did, wouldn't you? May we, like him, work hard while we can to master the fine art of imitating Jesus in all we do and say.

On Christlikeness

Watching Honesty Grow

As you think about the people around you in your life, is there one particular quality or attribute they exhibit that you value above others? I suspect there is for me – and that quality is honesty or integrity. I like to know people are undivided, that they say what they mean and mean what they say, and that there is no duplicity going on anywhere.

Perhaps you can therefore imagine how, when I first saw the plant *lunaria* or 'honesty', as it is commonly called, in a friend's garden a few years ago, I desperately wanted to grow it in my own garden too. I was duly given a few seedlings and, to my surprise, they survived, eventually developing into tall plants with large, dark-green leaves and beautiful, purple flowers.

I loved watching my honesty grow, flourish and burst into bloom. To me, this was like witnessing a real-life parable unfolding before my eyes, albeit a challenging one. But it was what happened subsequently that I loved even more. As the flowers and plants themselves began to die, the dry stems and oval-shaped seed pods remained. After some trial and error, I discovered how to gently remove the outer skin of the seed pods so as to allow the translucent, pearly, inner membrane to remain attached to the stems. I then placed these stems with their seed pods in a large vase in our lounge as a unique, home-grown, dried arrangement. There they stayed for many years, reminding me of the importance of maintaining integrity in my life.

It can be so easy, I find, to opt for half-truths in order to get ourselves out of a sticky situation or make ourselves look better than others. Some time back, during a challenging phone conversation with a business associate, I was left wondering whether to trust his word about anything as he tried to explain

On Christlikeness

away various broken promises, then vowed to do better in future. I found it all so disquieting – particularly since this person identified as a Christian. But I know within myself how tempting it can be to pretend to have more holiness, wisdom or integrity than I actually possess. As Jesus once pointed out, it is easy to judge others yet refuse to take a look at ourselves:

You hypocrite, first take the plank out of your own eye, and then you will see clearly to remove the speck from your brother's eye.

Matthew 7:5

Jesus did not mince words when it came to hypocrisy. On another occasion he said: 'Woe to you, teachers of the law and Pharisees, you hypocrites! You are like whitewashed tombs, which look beautiful on the outside but on the inside are full of the bones of the dead and everything unclean. In the same way, on the outside you appear to people as righteous but on the inside you are full of hypocrisy and wickedness' (Matthew 23:27–8).

Somehow, I get the picture that Jesus values honesty and integrity highly and considers it vital that what we say matches up with how we live and act. Is that what you think too?

Like those seed pods in my dried honesty arrangement, may our lives remain open and translucent at all times so that our integrity can shine through and bring honour and praise to God.

On Christlikeness

Big Shoes to Fill

I never cease to be amazed at the fresh discoveries I make each time I read the gospels. When I least expect it, God ambushes me with some truth that leaves me almost breathless with its clear, profound challenge.

One day while reading John's Gospel, I came to the following:

The evening meal was in progress, and the devil had already prompted Judas, the son of Simon Iscariot, to betray Jesus. Jesus knew that the Father had put all things under his power, and that he had come from God and was returning to God; so he got up from the meal, took off his outer clothing, and wrapped a towel round his waist. After that, he poured water into a basin and began to wash his disciples' feet, drying them with the towel that was wrapped round him.

John 13:2–5

My mouth fell open as I registered the massive contrast contained in these words. Jesus knows full well who he is and that his Father God has given him all power and authority. Yet, in obedience to his Father's will, he chooses to strip down, wrap a towel around himself and undertake the humble task of washing his disciples' dirty feet. It is almost too shocking to take in – I can well relate to Peter when he objects strongly to the whole idea (verses 6–10).

Even as I began to think how this could apply in my own life, I read on and saw how Jesus himself makes this all too clear:

I have set you an example that you should do as I have done for you. Very truly I tell you, no servant is greater than his master, nor is a messenger greater than the one who sent him. Now that you know these things, you will be blessed if you do them.

John 13:15–17

On Christlikeness

What a bitter pill for me to swallow. Was I *really* prepared to negate myself like that and serve others? I wanted to do much more interesting, exciting things than washing dirty feet, cleaning up after others or helping behind the scenes where my efforts would not be recognised. Yet Jesus says we are blessed if we do these things.

Then as God's Spirit gently but firmly wrestled with my rebellious spirit, I began to understand. Jesus knew who he was, where he came from and where he was going. No one could take those truths away from him. Because of Jesus, I can live my life with this same sure knowledge. I know I am God's precious child, totally loved, forgiven and accepted through Jesus. I know I am created in God's image and have been recreated through faith in Jesus – and I also know God has a place prepared for me in heaven for eternity.

In the light of all this, is it *really* such a problem to choose to serve others as Jesus did? How does the highest honour in this world compare with the privilege of spending eternity with God? I may well, in theory at least, write the greatest book ever, but if I lose my servant heart, the heart that Jesus had, then it is all meaningless.

Right now, I am heading off to find a towel to wrap around my waist. Would you like to join me?

On Christlikeness

Lessons from Long Ago

It was 1968 and I was in my busy, final year at university but decided I could not miss out on being a counsellor at the Billy Graham Crusade. This involved attendance at several training sessions and as many crusade meetings as possible. I was new to it all and, during this whole experience, learnt many unforgettable lessons.

For our training, we memorised key Bible verses to use when counselling, including Romans 3:23; Romans 6:23; John 3:16; John 1:12 and Ephesians 2:8–9. To this day, these verses remain imprinted on my mind. But I also learnt a huge lesson in grace during that training. Some, it seemed, were questioning others' fitness to be counsellors because they were not baptised or did not celebrate communion or did not adhere to some other church practice these critics regarded as essential. I remember well the gracious way our trainer spoke as he gently dealt with this matter and warned us all against being too judgemental.

Our trainer then asked if any of us had put into practice what we had learnt the previous week about sharing Christ with others. There was silence – until a little, old, Salvation Army lady stood up and, with a beaming face, told how she had talked about Jesus with someone on the train that very morning. What a profound, salutary lesson for all of us. This lady represented a group of Christians who do not usually practise baptism or take communion, yet apparently she was the only one who had shared Christ with someone that week.

But I was to learn an even more profound lesson about judging others one Sunday afternoon at the crusade itself. I had made my way to a popular

section of the large, open-air venue and was waiting for the meeting to begin. Two men sat in front of me, one of them smoking. I could tell this man was nervous – he fidgeted around as his friend tried to put him at ease. Then a man wearing an usher's badge approached them, red in the face.

'Excuse me,' he said loudly to the man smoking. 'Would you please put your cigarette out? This is a *religious* meeting!'

The man seemed stunned but apologised and did as he was asked.

Immediately, I wanted to punch that usher. I could not believe what I had witnessed. After all, we were seated in the open air – and no one else seemed to mind that the man was smoking. At least he was there, I fumed inwardly. I could feel the deep embarrassment of both poor men seated in front of me and suspected neither would hear a thing Billy Graham said that day because of that officious usher. Surely he could have been more discerning and prayed quietly for the man instead? Surely he could have remembered that the gospel is all about grace, as Ephesians 2:8–9 clearly states, and shown more of it himself?

Yes, I needed to be gracious too towards that usher who may truly have been offended. But may we all learn to mirror God's amazing grace to others at all times rather than alienate them with words of judgement.

Let your conversation be always full of grace, seasoned with salt, so that you may know how to answer everyone.

Colossians 4:6

On Christlikeness

Gulp!

Recently, I found myself in an interesting situation. For some time, I had stood talking with someone who was trying to be helpful and share her knowledge with me. Yet, inwardly, I was feeling rather annoyed, if not downright incensed, even though I realised this was hardly her fault. She did not know my background, after all. Much better to close my mouth and simply listen.

I tried to be polite and remember that this person meant well but, as time went by, I found it increasingly difficult. I attempted to interrupt her a few times as she continued giving me advice but, alas, my words fell on deaf ears. Could she not consider for a moment that she might be underestimating me? I already knew all the things she was telling me. I had been putting them into practice for years and had even trained others to do the same. In fact, I was willing to bet I knew much *more* than she did – or even others she had suggested might be able to help me. How dare this person think I was such an ignoramus?

In the end, I decided to show her what I knew. So, when she at last drew breath, I swooped and did just that. She smiled at me in a gracious manner, but it was obvious she did not believe me at all and still considered herself the expert.

For days afterwards, I hung on to my annoyance and wounded pride. I did not like being misjudged. I did not like my knowledge and experience being questioned or downright disbelieved. I did not like feeling so patronised. I knew there was nothing I could do about it, but it still rankled – a lot.

On Christlikeness

Then one morning, I opened my Bible and found I was up to Matthew 3, the account of John the Baptist's ministry. As I read, I was once again moved by the amazing courage and commitment John the Baptist showed in his honest, straightforward preaching and in the way he lived. How humble he was too, declaring he was merely the forerunner of someone much greater: 'I baptise you with water for repentance. But after me comes one who is more powerful than I, whose sandals I am not worthy to carry. He will baptise you with the Holy Spirit and fire' (Matthew 3:11).

Finally, I came to the account of Jesus' baptism. I tried to put myself right there in the scene and soon sensed what a huge moment of humility this was for both John the Baptist and Jesus. On the one hand, here was John the Baptist, blurting out how inadequate he felt being asked to baptise someone so much greater than he himself: 'I need to be baptised by you, and do you come to me?' (verse 14). On the other hand, here was Jesus, the sinless Son of God, humbly responding: 'Let it be so now; it is proper for us to do this to fulfil all righteousness' (verse 15).

At that point, I swallowed hard. Where was this same, wonderful humility in the way I had responded to the person a few days earlier who, after all, was only trying to help me?

Gulp! I think I got the message that morning. May we all take it to heart – and endeavour to put it into practice.

On Christlikeness

The Things We Know

I had obviously failed bigtime in our grandson's eyes. There he was, excitedly commenting on his favourite superhero characters in a puzzle book I had given him while I stood beside him, blank and befuddled. I know my basic superheroes like Spiderman, Iron Man and the Hulk but, alas, there were so many others I did not recognise. As for how they ended up with their various superpowers, it was obvious to our 8-year-old grandson that I did not have the foggiest idea.

'What? Don't you know *anything*, Nanna? *Everyone* knows that,' he told me in a tone dripping with disgust as he launched into an exasperated explanation of how Spiderman came to be Spiderman and the Hulk came to be . . . well, hulky.

Later that day as I sat eating dinner with our granddaughter, she suggested we might watch something on YouTube at the same time.

'I like this show,' she told me. 'It tells you what to do in an emergency, like when there's an earthquake or someone gets hurt. You'd better watch it too, Nanna, because you don't *know*!'

Hmm. Once again, I seemed to be a dismal failure, at least in a 6-year-old's eyes. So much for my two university degrees and two diplomas.

Later, I remembered a response I learnt as a child that might have come in handy in both these instances when our grandchildren seemed to decide I know nothing. It originated from something that happened during my mother's own growing-up years. There were seven children in her family,

the youngest being a boy. One day when he was still quite little, his older siblings teased him about something he did not know or understand. So to put them in their place, his response apparently went something like this, 'Well, I don't care anyway. I only just know a *good couple* of things.'

At my stage of life, I think I can say without too much pride that I know a 'good couple of things' in some areas at least, as I am sure you also do. Yet there is so much more I would love to know. I would love to explore and appreciate many more great works of literature, art and classical music. I would love to be able to paint – and I would love to learn how to play the violin and cello.

I wonder what things you would like to explore more or be able to do. Yet whatever knowledge or skills we may gain, one day these will all need to be put aside, won't they? One day, the only thing that will matter will be whether we know Jesus, the one 'in whom are hidden all the treasures of wisdom and knowledge' (Colossians 2:3). This is the only knowing that can truly satisfy us deep down and enable us to stand tall, whatever knowledge or skills we might lack in others' eyes.

May we all, with complete honesty and humble certainty, be ready and able to echo the words of the Apostle Paul when our time here on earth is done:

I know the one in whom I trust, and I am sure that he is able to guard what I have entrusted to him until the day of his return.

2 Timothy 1:12, NLT

On Christlikeness

How Wrong Could I Be?

One day, I spent some hours promoting my books at our local, Christian bookstore. The time flew by but, at one stage, I decided to sit down and have a brief break from connecting with customers. Earlier, I had eaten a hurried lunch and had tried to buy a coffee but had given up because the store café was so busy. Now, however, more than anything else, I wanted that nice, hot cup of coffee to help keep me going.

Soon after, I noticed a middle-aged couple browsing nearby. For a moment, I thought of getting up and chatting with them but decided against it. I was too tired. Besides, they did not look like the sort of people who might be interested in my books. The man seemed quite serious and already had a pile of other books under his arm while the lady appeared somewhat vague to me and . . . well, just a little quaint.

Soon, however, they came closer and eventually ended up right in front of my book table. I explained a few things about my books to them as politely as I could, but then the gentleman looked straight at me and said in his rather loud voice, 'Do you need anything? What can I get you?'

'Oh, nothing – I'm fine,' I lied. 'I wouldn't want to bother you anyway, but thank you.'

'No, no,' the man insisted. 'It would be our privilege to serve you. What would you like? Some water perhaps? Or a soda or coffee?'

I could not resist at that point. 'To be honest,' I admitted, 'I would truly love a coffee. I've tried to buy one twice today already but the staff were too busy and I had to get back here to my book table.'

On Christlikeness

'Our pleasure. What sort of coffee? Milk? Sugar?'

Feeling humbled and more than a little embarrassed, I gave them my order and off they went.

Not long after, they returned, coffee in hand, and I almost burst into tears.

'Wow, you are such lifesavers,' I told them – and truly meant it.

We chatted for a while then and, in the end, the man's wife happily bought one of my novels, which humbled me even more.

Afterwards, as I sat sipping my wonderful, hot coffee, I sensed God whispering gently, 'See, Jo-Anne? They *wanted* to do that for you. There is no shame in acknowledging your need, and it gave them joy too. But . . . don't judge so quickly next time, will you?

As I watched this lovely couple leave the store, I saw them afresh with God's eyes and thanked God for their soft, servant hearts. They had treated me, a complete stranger, in exactly the way Paul urges us to treat others:

You, my brothers and sisters, were called to be free. But do not use your freedom to indulge the flesh; rather, serve one another humbly in love.
Galatians 5:13

In the process, unbeknown to them, the couple had taught me more than one vitally important lesson. They showed me I must not be too proud to acknowledge my needs to God and others – and they certainly taught me to be far less judgemental all round.

May God help us all to become more and more like them each day.

On Christlikeness

One Little Word

Several years ago, a certain notable event in our family caused me to think carefully about the enormous power one little word in our English language can wield. It is a word that often sticks in our throats and becomes hard to ever contemplate saying because the stakes may seem too high to us. Yes – it is that one little word, 'sorry'.

It seems this word is hard even for 2-year-olds to say – or at least it was for our little grandson. While visiting us one day, he did something naughty and, as a result, his father took him on his knee and decided his son needed to say sorry. But this was not an option our grandson was prepared to consider for a moment. Instead, he sat there, shaking his head and refusing to say that one little word that would defuse the whole situation. How could he, a 2-year-old, know how to be so stubborn? What might have caused him to decide he was not prepared to stoop so low as to apologise?

At that point, rightly or wrongly, his conflict-avoidance grandmother decided to resort to bribery and offered him a lollipop if he would say sorry. But even that did not change his mind. When his father began to eat that lollipop instead, there were great cries of anguish – but still no 'sorry'. The lollipop slowly grew smaller and smaller until it had almost disappeared. But that little word was never said.

A few days later, our grandson said to his mother out of the blue, 'Lollipops at Nanna's house. But I didn't get one. I didn't say sorry.'

So he had understood what the issue was and how high the stakes were. After all, a lollipop is a big deal to a 2-year-old.

On Forgiveness

What about us, however, when it comes to saying that one little word? How mature are we in such a situation? What happens when we know we need to tell God we are sorry? There is much more than a lollipop at stake in this instance, yet I, like my grandson, so often seem to have too much pride and stubbornness to admit my faults, even to our loving, forgiving God. On top of that, I seem to have an endless, inbuilt supply of excuses ready as to why I do not need to admit to falling so far short of how God would want me to behave:

'It doesn't matter.'

'God will forgive me anyway.'

'It wasn't so bad, after all.'

'Others have done much worse than I have.'

'I'm too ashamed – I don't even want to think about it.'

I hope I grow up one day. I hope I wake up to myself soon and remember how important it is to keep short accounts with God. I hope I never forget the freedom forgiveness brings when we come before our loving Father with contrite hearts just as the lost son Jesus spoke about did when he returned home (Luke 15).

Is 'sorry' hard for you to say too – especially to God?

If we claim to be without sin, we deceive ourselves and the truth is not in us. If we confess our sins, he is faithful and just and will forgive us our sins and purify us from all unrighteousness.

1 John 1:8–9

On Forgiveness

Such a Shame

I am sure I have managed to embarrass quite a few people in my life. I can recall several occasions when my parents ended up rather red-faced over something I had done – and I am sure I can remember times when my children let me know how much I had embarrassed them in one way or another.

I am also good at embarrassing myself. Nowadays, I can laugh more readily at the silly things I do, but there was a time when I was much more sensitive and prone to feeling ashamed after I had goofed in some way. I always found it shameful too when challenged about something I had said or done. As a child, I hated it whenever my parents disciplined me – it was altogether too humiliating and embarrassing. Whenever they did, I would curl up in a ball with my thumb in my mouth. 'I'm *not* a naughty girl!' I would sob, heartbroken.

I think I understand the insidious nature of shame. It can become all-pervading and was something I eventually had to ask God to help me deal with. Then one day, I stumbled upon a further challenging insight into this whole matter from God's perspective. At the time, I was reading through Hebrews 11, where the writer describes the exploits of godly people in the past and how they were commended for their faith. There I was, enjoying being reminded of these men and women when I came to a verse that shocked me: 'Instead, they were longing for a better country – a heavenly one. Therefore God is not ashamed to be called their God, for he has prepared a city for them' (Hebrews 11:16).

On Forgiveness

If God was not ashamed to be known as the God of these heroes of the faith, then that must mean God could well have been ashamed of others who did *not* persevere, I reasoned. So could that happen now? Could that even perhaps apply to me? What a horrifying thought! I would never, ever want to embarrass God. But . . . what about the times I put other things before God in my life? What about when I dishonour God by not mentioning my faith in Jesus? What about those angry, critical comments I blurt out at times? What about those occasions when I do not trust God will provide for me and, instead, give in to my doubts and fears? What about the way I so often live like an orphan instead of a much-loved child of the King? Could these things ever cause God to be ashamed of me?

How wonderful it is that God is so forgiving and so gracious because of Jesus' sacrifice for us all. How amazing that God continues to love me, at the same time as possibly feeling ashamed of my behaviour. How thankful I am that God is able to lift any guilt and shame off me and replace it with perfect love and acceptance – forever.

I, even I, am he who blots out
your transgressions, for my own sake,
and remembers your sins no more.

Isaiah 43:25

In return, my heart's desire is to walk in the wonderful freedom of God's forgiveness and to bring honour rather than shame to God's name. May that truly be your heart's desire too.

On Forgiveness

Quick . . . Slow . . . Slow

It was only a small difference of opinion at first. I was sure I had remembered to explain everything about something I had done, but it soon became obvious that the person involved had not heard me at all. Or perhaps it was that I *thought* I had said things clearly but, instead, those thoughts had never actually been spoken aloud. Whatever the case, I was tired and cross – and I did not want to entertain the quite reasonable possibility that this difference of opinion was my fault. So casting caution to the wind, I stuck to my guns and maintained I had in fact explained everything well. I argued my case with vehemence. With great fervour, I maintained I was right. In my anger and frustration at being unjustly accused, I might even have raised my voice significantly. All in order to defend myself over something that did not matter greatly in the bigger scheme of things.

Later that day, shame at my response kicked in, but my anger at being wrongfully accused remained. Why did I have to apologise when I knew I had been right? Better just to let things die down. It would probably all blow over by tomorrow anyway. Yet something nagged at my conscience – and some words that had always made complete sense to me in the past kept coming to mind:

Do not let the sun go down while you are still angry, and do not give the devil a foothold.

Ephesians 4:26–7

So at last I apologised – and my apology was accepted with grace. We talked a little about how much better it is to let differences of opinion over trivial issues go rather than try to justify ourselves, then left it at that.

On Forgiveness

But I soon discovered God had not finished dealing with the issue. Still feeling a little disgruntled, I sat at my desk and picked up a book of devotionals someone had given me a few days earlier. I turned to the reading for the day and almost laughed out loud, despite my negative attitude. Right at the top, printed in bold, red letters, was James 1:19b–20: 'Everyone should be quick to listen, slow to speak and slow to become angry, because human anger does not produce the righteousness that God desires.'

I wonder if these words are as strong a challenge to you as they have always been to me. Somehow, that order of 'quick . . . slow . . . slow' can so easily be reversed, can't it? Often, I am much more likely to be *slow* to listen, *quick* to speak and *quick* to become angry as I rush to defend myself. In fact, I may not even hear what the other person is trying to tell me before I crank up the volume and start talking, sometimes over the top of them.

Hopefully, I am slowly learning to take a deep breath, hold back and give the other person a chance to say what is troubling them. Hopefully, one day soon, I will improve as I model myself more on how God has treated me – and still does on a daily basis:

But you, Lord, are a compassionate and gracious God,
    slow to anger, abounding in love and faithfulness.

Psalm 86:15

On Forgiveness

Honey Fixes Everything

I love it when someone tells me about an event in their lives that they can now honestly laugh about even though it may have caused them pain at the time. It is as if they have chosen to step through a doorway into a place of much greater freedom, joy and light rather than remain stuck in some dark cell, enmeshed in anger, bitterness and confusion.

Recently, it was a privilege to hear one such amazing story from a good friend. How special it was to laugh with her as she shared something that happened to her during a trip home to Korea to see her aging father and other family members. Yet it was even more special to sense the freedom she now feels about it all and to share in her joy that she was able to respond to this situation with true, God-given wisdom and strength.

While back in Korea, my friend discovered her aging father had caused a huge difference of opinion among their extended family members. My friend has six aunts in Korea – surely a formidable force to contend with anywhere – and all of them were angry with her father because they felt a certain choice he had made dishonoured the memory of her mother who had passed away some years earlier. So what was she to do? She had loved her mother – but she also loves her 86-year-old father and wants his final years to be as pleasant as possible. How could she honour her father's wishes but also honour her six aunts?

In the end, she took her father's side and talked firmly to her aunts, one by one, urging them to leave him alone and not be angry with him. She reminded them that, as his daughter, she is his closest relative and that

On Forgiveness

they therefore needed to abide by her decision as well as his. She handled it bravely and well, I believe. But she went even further.

You see, when my friend arrived back home in Australia, she bought a large tin of honey for each aunt and posted it to them as a gift. Honey is expensive enough in itself, even without adding the high cost of postage. Yes, there is honey in Korea, but it is apparently not as thick as ours, so this was a precious gift indeed to send them. They were all delighted – and, as a result, their difference of opinion was swept under the carpet and forgotten.

'So . . . honey fixes everything,' my friend told me, laughing. 'It is "supernatural food"!'

It is indeed, don't you think? To me, it symbolises a sweet response that went far beyond our natural inclination to argue and defend and hold a grudge, speaking instead of the supernatural responses of forbearance, of forgiveness in God's strength and of wise peace-making. This is in fact how we are all called to live.

Turn from evil and do good;
  seek peace and pursue it.

Psalm 34:14

Bear with each other and forgive one another if any of you has a grievance against someone. Forgive as the Lord forgave you.

Colossians 3:13

Perhaps we should all consider sharing this 'supernatural food' around a little more often and see for ourselves how honey truly does fix everything.

On Forgiveness

Picking Up Where We Left Off

There I was, slowly wending my way through my latest manuscript yet again, checking for errors and polishing it up as best I could. It was painstaking work and seemed to go on forever. But each morning as I went to my laptop and reopened the relevant document to work on it again, I felt cheered on by the polite, little greeting awaiting me there. Again and again, a little box would pop up on the right of my screen and declare happily, 'Welcome back! Pick up where you left off.'

How encouraging is that? But one day, that little message did more than cheer me up and increase my determination to pick up where I left off. This time around, there seemed to be something extra in the words I read there. It was as if God had highlighted that little box on my screen on purpose that day so I would not miss out on the special, deeper message it contained just for me.

In an instant, I sensed God saying, 'That's exactly what I've said to you so many times over the years, Jo-Anne. Whenever you have turned around and repented, after pulling back from me and going your own way, I have always been there, waiting for you with open arms. Time and time again, like your laptop does each day, I have said to you, "Welcome back! Pick up where you left off." What a joy it has been to offer you my forgiveness – how good it has been to pick you up and help you stand firm again.'

As I took in God's gracious message to me, I recalled the Apostle Peter's own story in Scripture. I love Peter. He seems to have been such a full-on person – always the leader, opening his mouth on behalf of the rest of the disciples and stepping out when others might well have been too afraid.

On Forgiveness

I love how he realises Jesus is the only one worth following and the only one who can offer eternal life: 'Lord, to whom shall we go? You have the words of eternal life. We have come to believe and to know that you are the Holy One of God' (John 6:68–9). I love how he is brave enough to step out and walk towards Jesus on the water (Matthew 14). I love too how he declares he will never deny Jesus, fully thinking that is true – and I always feel sad when I read how he does exactly that, then weeps bitterly (Matthew 26:75). But later, when the resurrected Jesus appears on the shore as Peter is fishing with the other disciples and proceeds to cook their breakfast, I hold my breath at what unfolds. Three times, Jesus asks Peter if he loves him – and three times, Peter replies: 'Lord, you know that I love you' (John 21:15–17).

Can you imagine how Peter must have felt as Jesus reinstated him in such a loving way and commissioned him to be the strong leader he had called him to be? What grace Jesus showed him that day – and what grace Jesus shows each of us today too as he reaches out in love and mercy and says to us whenever we return to him, 'Welcome back! Pick up where you left off.'

On Forgiveness

Feline Reflections

Some years ago, our daughter asked us to look after her cat for a few days. Now Panda (the cat) was 16 years old at that point and not as agile as she once was. She stalked somewhat disdainfully around our house, thinking twice before trying to jump up anywhere. Then when given the freedom of our backyard, she tentatively explored it a little but soon settled down in a favourite spot under a tree. She has always been choosy about whom she selects as a trustworthy friend and did not seem overly enamoured with either my husband or me. But from around 5.30 p.m. onwards, she seemed to treat me as her best buddy, brushing up against my legs and meowing plaintively. I hated to doubt her motives, but I suspect it could have had something to do with the fact that it was almost her dinner-time.

Then it dawned on me that Panda might well be enacting a real-life parable before my eyes. Could her behaviour perhaps replicate some of my less-than-honourable attitudes? For a start, could the fact that she did not seem to care much about me most of the day but changed her mind at dinner-time perhaps mirror my behaviour towards God on occasions? Surely this is what I do when I turn to God only when I need something?

I noticed another even more disquieting way in which Panda might mirror my own behaviour. She appeared to be a lovely, old cat, just waiting for you to pat her or pick her up and sit her on your lap. But in reality, she was quite unfriendly – with most people anyway. At times, she would even hiss and lash out at any pesky humans who annoyed her. Could I possibly resemble Panda in this way too? How often do I pretend to be much more righteous and holy and . . . well . . . nicer than I really am? Yet I never fool God for

On Forgiveness

one minute. God sees past it all, right into my heart – but, amazingly, still loves and accepts me anyway.

Then there was the certain knowledge that, in a couple of days when our daughter came to reclaim her pet, Panda would speedily switch her allegiance from me back to her owner. How could my feline friend be so fickle after all I had done for her – cleaning out her litter tray, providing her favourite, gourmet, salmon dinners, stroking her when she deigned to let me, removing all her hairs from my best lounge chair? Yet am I perhaps just as fickle as that with God? Do I perhaps regularly switch my allegiance from God to whatever else will bring me pleasure and fulfilment?

I am so thankful God is much more gracious and loving with me than I ever was with Panda. I am so glad God cares enough to forgive my pretence and my ever-changing allegiances and helps me do better. I hope I learnt much from caring for Panda – including being able to echo King David's honest prayer with equal honesty in my own heart:

Search me, God, and know my heart;
   test me and know my anxious thoughts.
See if there is any offensive way in me,
   and lead me in the way everlasting.

Psalm 139:23–4

On Forgiveness

Making Mistakes

While minding our 4-year-old granddaughter one day, I began to wonder whether she was indeed only 4 and not 104. We were sitting on the floor, trying to set up some wooden train tracks together. I knew they were meant to form three intertwining loops yet, whatever I did, I could not make them do what they were supposed to do.

'Oh dear,' I said to our granddaughter, 'I think I've made a big mistake. These tracks aren't connecting up at all.'

Thankfully, she did not express any frustration at my failure. 'Don't worry, Nanna,' she said in her lovely, compassionate way. 'Everyone makes mistakes. *Everyone!* . . . Even *I* made a mistake once.'

I tried not to laugh because I knew she would be highly offended if I did. Besides, she had meant it all kindly and there was so much wisdom in her initial words at least. As for her final sentence, it had been shared with a good heart to help me feel better about myself.

At that point, I let her know I truly appreciated what she had said. In fact, in a weird way, I was comforted by her words because I had indeed felt a little silly that I could not put a simple train track together. Eventually, I found some instructions in the accompanying box and, after my husband decided to take our granddaughter to the playground for a while, I managed to put those pesky train tracks together. What a sense of accomplishment I felt as I did!

On Forgiveness

Our granddaughter's loving response also caused me to reflect on the many much more serious mistakes I have made in my life. Sometimes, I have said or done things out of ignorance, thinking I was right and, in fact, even believing I was acting in a godly manner. On these occasions, God has known my heart, seen my sorrow, graciously picked me up and enabled me to do better.

On other occasions, however, to my regret, I have deliberately chosen a wrong course of action, knowing full well I am making a huge mistake – in other words, sinning. Many times, I have judged someone harshly or spat out a hasty, angry word, refusing to listen when God has prompted me to speak merciful, life-giving words instead. Yet each time, God has reached out to me, shown me my mistakes and, in kindness, set my feet on solid ground once again as I have repented (Romans 2:4). Truly, our God is so loving, patient and forbearing.

The LORD is compassionate and gracious,
    slow to anger, abounding in love.
He will not always accuse,
    nor will he harbour his anger for ever;
he does not treat us as our sins deserve
    or repay us according to our iniquities.
For as high as the heavens are above the earth,
    so great is his love for those who fear him;
as far as the east is from the west,
    so far has he removed our transgressions from us.

Psalm 103:8–12

Sadly, our granddaughter is bound to make more than one mistake in her lifetime. But I hope and pray she will know her loving, compassionate Lord is always close by to forgive her, comfort her and help her move forward again in his strength – and I hope and pray you do too.

On Forgiveness

The Flow-on Effect

It is amazing how so many opinions and discussions, uplifting or otherwise, can fly around the world very quickly on the internet via such public platforms as Facebook, isn't it? In a trice, someone can respond to a post with a pleasant or unpleasant comment, and a whole prolonged conversation can ensue. Just a few little words, yet they can rapidly become a stream or river – or even a torrent.

Sometimes, these online conversations can become undignified and even vicious. At other times, people are kind and courteous, wanting to build up rather than tear down – and I am convinced God can use these positive exchanges in ways we would never imagine. In fact, I think God might have even smiled at one I became involved in recently as it unfolded.

It began when our son shared the words of Proverbs 16:24 on Facebook from his home in Sydney, together with an image of honey dripping from a piece of honeycomb.

Gracious words are a honeycomb,
   sweet to the soul and healing to the bones.

Proverbs 16:24

These words are well worth pondering, I thought – and that is exactly what one of our daughters decided too. But then she had an honest question, which she proceeded to share on her brother's post from her home on the other side of Sydney. How *can* kind words actually bring healing to our bones? Our son responded that he was unsure but hoped someone else out there would know.

As I thought about our daughter's question, several ideas came to mind. Kind words certainly make us *feel* good, just like that burst of sweetness from honey does. We seem to relax inside when we realise someone appreciates us, don't we? We feel connected to them too, heart to heart or spirit to spirit. I also vaguely remembered reading how honey was used in times past as an antiseptic on an open wound – and I knew some people drink honey and lemon juice to soothe sore throats and help counteract flu symptoms. Then, after checking online, I discovered honey and lemon juice can apparently aid our digestion, flush out toxins from the body and even stop us putting on weight! So . . . could gracious words have a similar healthy effect?

Delving further online, I read that, as we experience someone's kindness, our bodies produce the hormone oxytocin. This then stimulates production of nitric oxide which, in turn, dilates our arteries and reduces blood pressure. As well, this oxytocin can act as an anti-inflammatory in our cardiovascular system, thus protecting our whole bodies. How amazing! Apparently, there is an actual scientific reason for those lovely, warm fuzzies we feel throughout our bodies when we hear a kind word from someone.

From yet another part of Sydney then, I decided to share these brief insights on our son's post in an attempt to answer his sister's question. Soon, others commented further, resulting in a flow of excellent, uplifting thoughts and information on the subject.

Through one brief quote online from Proverbs, a whole group of people across Sydney and beyond were eventually connected heart-to-heart and built up in a wonderful, unique way. May we all look for more opportunities to enable others to experience similar encouraging, grace-filled flow-on effects – and may God's Spirit flow through all our words as we do.

On Encouragement and Comfort

Hearing Our Name

I wonder if you like the sound of your own name. Often, it can depend on who is saying it, can't it? If it is an irate schoolteacher rebuking us for some misdemeanour, our name might grate on us a little. But if it is a good friend greeting us after not having seen us for some time, that might be a different matter.

I look forward to hearing my name spoken whenever I phone a good friend. 'Hello, Jo-Anne – how lovely to hear your voice again. How *are* you?' she always says with such unfeigned joy and delight that my heart melts. I also remember how, many years ago, a young minister at our church went to the trouble of asking me whether I preferred to be called 'Jo' or 'Jo-Anne'. I honestly do not mind being called 'Jo', which is what my husband and almost everyone else have called me for years. But I told him I preferred 'Jo-Anne' because it seems just that bit softer and more feminine to me. From that point on, the minister tried hard to remember to call me that. Whenever he did, I was touched by his thoughtfulness and always felt respected by him as a result.

I think of this experience whenever I read the account of Jesus' resurrection in John 20. I often like to imagine myself right in the middle of the scene at the tomb when Mary Magdalene discovers Jesus is no longer there. She is devastated because she believes someone has taken his body and, in her distress, does not immediately recognise Jesus when he speaks to her. But what a moment that must have been when she heard him say that one word that must have told her so much – 'Mary' (20:16a).

Can you imagine that moment? I wonder what tone of voice Jesus used when speaking her name. Was it soft and tender? Or was it loud and commanding, as Jesus sought to make Mary realise who he was? Did it convey joy and delight that she had come, wanting to attend to his body? Did it show something of his pride in her that she was faithful to the end? Perhaps it conveyed trust as well because, as soon as Mary realises who he is, Jesus proceeds to give her a message for the other disciples: 'Do not hold on to me, for I have not yet ascended to the Father. Go instead to my brothers and tell them, "I am ascending to my Father and your Father, to my God and your God"' (John 20:17).

One thing I know for sure is that Jesus' voice was filled with amazing love for Mary when he spoke her name. Today, Jesus still speaks our names in that same loving tone as he calls us back into relationship with our heavenly Father and into the family of God. How privileged we are that he knows our names and that we too can hear him speaking to us just as the Israelites did long ago, calling us, guiding us and strengthening us day by day.

But now, this is what the LORD says –
   he who created you, Jacob,
   he who formed you, Israel:
'Do not fear, for I have redeemed you;
   I have summoned you by name; you are mine.'

Isaiah 43:1

On Encouragement and Comfort

Finding Out What God Is Up To

Some time back, I found myself in complaining mode yet again as a result of the pressure of too many ongoing commitments in my life and too much involvement in numerous one-off, unforeseen activities, large and small. For the most part, I stewed in silence. But then, after venting my feelings to someone at great length, I began to surface from my morass of self-pity and see things in a more reasonable light.

Yes, I decided, I had a right to complain about some unexpected things that had occurred and some decisions others had made that impacted me in a negative way. I was justified in feeling a little imposed upon. As for some of the ongoing situations, I decided it was okay and, in fact, important to be honest and acknowledge the difficulty these were causing me. But what should my response be from this point on? What was the best, godly way forward for me through it all? You see, at last it had dawned on me that God was still there in the midst of everything. God knew all my mixed emotions and muddled thoughts. Not only that, God still loved me with the most amazing, tender, caring love and wanted me to remember that.

But how did I manage to reach this conclusion? First, I believe God calmed me down enough to recognise the Spirit's gentle voice, whispering this truth to me. Second, I received a beautiful email from a friend who told me she was praying for God's encouragement and love to surround me and wanted to share with me some special words from Ephesians:

Long before he laid down earth's foundations, he had us in mind, had settled on us as the focus of his love, to be made whole and holy by his love. Long, long ago he decided to adopt us into his family through Jesus Christ. (What

pleasure he took in planning this!) He wanted us to enter into the celebration of his lavish gift-giving by the hand of his beloved Son.

Ephesians 1:4–6, MSG

I had a clear choice at that point. I could continue to grumble and stew and feel sorry for myself, ignoring what God might be saying to me through these words of Scripture – and indeed through the situations in my life and my responses to them. Or I could change my focus, step back a little and allow God to widen my perspective and show me the wisest way forward through it all. A 'no-brainer', wouldn't you agree?

For a while at least, it had somehow slipped my mind that, because God's Spirit lives in me, just as was promised to Jesus' disciples, then God is an integral part of everything in my life (John 14:16–17). Nothing takes God by surprise – and God is quite able to use every situation to teach us something and draw us even closer. Surely then, my best response at that stage was to relax in my heavenly Father's loving arms, receive the grace and mercy that is always available to me and choose to listen once again to the Spirit's voice.

God is always up to something in our lives, something wise, good and wonderful. May we all give thanks for and rejoice in this amazing truth.

On Encouragement and Comfort

Higher Ways

Can you remember a time when you went somewhere with a particular purpose in mind, only to find God had some surprises lined up for you – or perhaps even an entirely different agenda? What was your initial response? Did you feel a little annoyed, as I have at times? After all, what could God be *thinking*, to mess up my plans!

Some time ago, an author friend and I arranged to promote our books at a Christian bookstore. Our day started well. On arrival, I found someone had already picked up one of my books and was waiting for me to sign it. He also insisted on having his photo taken with us and, for a few seconds at least, we felt like minor celebrities. Things were a little slow after that, but we still had some good conversations with customers and sold a few books. Anyway, there was always hope it would become busier after lunch. At that stage, however, we had no idea of the special experiences God had in store for us.

Our first 'God surprise' came via a friendly man and his disabled teenage son who was in a wheelchair. I chatted briefly with them both, before moving off to talk to someone else. When I returned to our book table, the man and his son were holding hands with my friend and praying for her. I silently joined in the prayer, feeling humbled that these beautiful people were so keen to pray for others. Later, I heard how the man's son had felt God wanted them to pray about a particular health issue with my friend so, after discovering this was indeed something she suffers from, they did exactly that. What amazing, compassionate people, so full of the light and love of God.

On Encouragement and Comfort

Then, when it was almost time for us to leave, a lady I had met several months earlier when I had last signed books in this same store came by. Soon after that first meeting, she and a friend had caught up with me for coffee during which I told them about some issues our grandson was having at school. Now as she greeted me warmly, her first words flabbergasted me.

'Hello, Jo-Anne – lovely to see you again. How is your little grandson? My friend and I have been praying for him by name that God will provide just the right resources for him.'

This beautiful lady, with so much else happening in her life, had gone on faithfully praying for our grandson throughout those intervening months. What is more, while I could not recall her name at first, she had remembered our grandson's name and was eager to hear how he was doing. Again, what a wonderful, humbling, encouraging 'God moment'.

Initially, I viewed these experiences as interruptions, but how wrong I was – and how much more amazing were the things God had planned for us. May we all be ready and willing to let go of our own agendas more often, trade our own thoughts for God's and enjoy exploring God's beautiful, higher ways instead.

'**For my thoughts are not your thoughts,**
   neither are your ways my ways,'
   declares the LORD.
'**As the heavens are higher than the earth,**
   so are my ways higher than your ways
   and my thoughts than your thoughts.'

Isaiah 55:8–9

On Encouragement and Comfort

Sharing the Joy

Have you noticed how wonderful it is to hear *good* news during times when bad news seems to hold sway everywhere? It can feel like beautiful, soothing ointment on a raw wound or a cool drink on a boiling hot day, can't it?

Recently, I received an excited text from a friend. She had just discovered she did not have to pay a certain bill she owed, which was for a sizeable amount. Way back, I had read something online that suggested she might not have to and had mentioned this to her. As soon as she could, she had investigated further and put her case to the relevant authorities. Many enquiries, pleasant/unpleasant phone calls and requests for various documents followed, but my friend did not give up. Now her perseverance had paid off.

In the midst of her relief, she felt she *had* to share her good news with me straight away – and I was so glad she did. At first, I could not believe something I had told her way back, without any great faith, had actually borne fruit. After all, I did not know much about the matter and am no expert when it comes to understanding government, financial technicalities. Yet it had happened. It was true – and the fact that God had used me, even in my ignorance, to play a small part in enabling my friend to receive this good news added to my joy.

Later, as I reflected on this whole event, I could not help thinking of Jesus' parables of the lost sheep and lost coin where he comments how natural it is for those involved to want to share their joy when their search pays off: 'Then he calls his friends and neighbours together and says, "Rejoice

with me; I have found my lost sheep"' (Luke 15:6); 'And when she finds it, she calls her friends and neighbours together and says, "Rejoice with me; I have found my lost coin"' (Luke 15:9).

That is exactly what my friend was doing via her text, I realised. How wonderful it was to rejoice together and laugh almost in disbelief over God's amazing grace and provision for her. But then I realised Jesus' aim in telling these stories was to point out something so much more wonderful than even that: 'I tell you that in the same way there will be more rejoicing in heaven over one sinner who repents' (Luke 15:7a); 'In the same way, I tell you, there is rejoicing in the presence of the angels of God over one sinner who repents' (Luke 15:10).

I marvelled then that, when I first came to experience the love and grace of God in my life and believed in Jesus with all my heart, joy erupted in heaven. Just as Jesus also taught in his parable about the lost son, there *had* to be a party held in heaven to celebrate the moment: 'But we had to celebrate and be glad, because this brother of yours was dead and is alive again; he was lost and is found' (Luke 15:32).

Wow! Imagine God celebrating my new birth with such joy in the same way as I now found myself celebrating my friend's good news. What an amazing reminder of how much I matter to God – and how much *you* do too.

On Encouragement and Comfort

Lightening the Load

I had just arrived to pick up our two youngest grandchildren from after-school care and needed to ensure we had everything. Two large backpacks? Tick. Two lunch boxes? Tick. Two water bottles? Tick. Two jumpers? Tick. Two pairs of shoes and socks? Well . . . almost. Only one pair of socks missing this time around – not too bad. Two children signed out? Tick. So off we headed to the car.

I managed to get everything in safely, children included, and drove off. A few minutes later, we were home. I proceeded to collect my own bags, get out of the car, undo our 3-year-old grandson's seat harness, steer him onto the footpath, then inspire him to stand still while I put his bag on his back.

'What a help you are to me today!' I told him as he obliged.

Then it was our granddaughter's turn to be extricated from her car seat. I decided she could walk the short distance to their apartment so went to pick up both her bag and mine and hold her hand. But she was having none of it. At 18 months, she managed to convey to me in no uncertain terms that she wanted to carry her *own* backpack, thank you very much. The only trouble was it was about as big as she was and also rather heavy.

For a few moments, she managed to stand more or less upright, then – thump – over she went backwards. It would have been funny if it had not been just that little bit cruel. At that point, I tried to take her bag off her, but she was still determined to refuse my offer. Instead, she hung on to it for dear life and yelled loudly. All I could do was walk along slowly beside her, trying to steady her and help when she fell over backwards yet again.

On Encouragement and Comfort

As I thought about this later, I began to wonder how many times I have done something similar in my own adult life. How often have I tried to carry a big, figurative backpack that was far too heavy for me? How often have I rejected help, wanting to do it all by myself? How often have I turned a deaf ear to God's gentle voice, showing me a better way forward, offering me a much lighter load to carry? How often have I worried and stressed too much over things when God was right there to ease my burden?

I wonder whether, right now, some of you might be needing to get rid of some heavy load that is causing you to struggle and stumble. Is it time for you to take Jesus' outstretched hand and allow him to help you move forward in his strength rather than in your own?

May your load soon be much lighter as you journey on with Jesus – and may you and I carry no more and no less than what he gives us to carry.

Come to me, all you who are weary and burdened, and I will give you rest. Take my yoke upon you and learn from me, for I am gentle and humble in heart, and you will find rest for your souls. For my yoke is easy and my burden is light.

Matthew 11:28–30

On Encouragement and Comfort

Facing the Day

Sometimes, it can be easier to get out of bed than others. Sometimes, we may not have slept well and truly need those extra minutes – or hours – in bed. Sometimes, our feelings may also depend on what our day will hold. If there is something exciting happening, we may well bound out of bed. But if we know we need to clean the house or do something else we dread, we may indeed want to hide under the blankets a while longer. Perhaps some of us may be facing even more daunting challenges, such as serious, ongoing health issues, relationship difficulties or grief at the loss of a loved one, all of which may drain the colour from our days.

Yes, sometimes it can take a while before we feel we can conquer whatever lies ahead for us – and, according to our personality or life situation, we may have different ways of tackling such a challenge. Some of us may decide to stick to a set routine in order to be able to function. We may like to have an early morning cup of coffee first or take a hot shower or eat breakfast, followed by working our way through some personal regimen we have devised. Then, as my husband declared recently, on completing his own meticulous morning routine, we may feel we can indeed say, 'Now I'm ready to face the day!' As for me, I am likely to be quite uncommunicative at first, perhaps even monosyllabic. Then I may fumble along in a haphazard way for a while until I can surface and fully gather my wits.

Years ago, we used to mind our oldest granddaughter each Friday. Her father would arrive on our doorstep around 7 a.m. and present this little, slightly sleepy, blonde-headed child to us, complete with all her gear, before heading off to his teaching job. We would cuddle her for a while before giving her breakfast and dressing her, by which time she would be

more awake. Then, when we ventured outside to play or go somewhere, she would often look up at the sky and say, 'Lovely day!' in such a cute way, just as her parents must have said to her often on leaving home.

Sometimes, however, we may find it impossible to call our day 'lovely' in any shape or form. Sometimes, it may well be a matter of bravely putting one foot in front of the other. On days like this, I have found it even more important to acknowledge my feelings honestly to God but also to remember that God is still there and still cares so much about me. How wonderful it is when, despite my attitude or circumstances, I can sense God's Spirit comforting me and filling me yet again. I know God is with me. I know God loves me. I know I can trust God, come what may.

Whatever life holds for you right now, may God enable you to take hold of these truths too and experience God's unfailing compassion for you each day.

Because of the LORD's great love we are not consumed,
   for his compassions never fail.
They are new every morning;
   great is your faithfulness.
I say to myself, 'The LORD is my portion;
   therefore I will wait for him.'

Lamentations 3:22–4

On Encouragement and Comfort

So Lonely

He was seated by himself at the end of the very front row in the room where I was soon scheduled to speak. I had arrived early to ensure my PowerPoint presentation worked at the venue so I was preoccupied at first. But when I had to wait for a staff member to assist me, the gentleman and I started chatting. I had already noticed how isolated he seemed to be – and I also noticed he was attached to an oxygen machine on his wheelchair.

I cannot remember how our conversation began, but it was not long before he told me, a complete stranger, that his wife of sixty-three years had passed away only a few months earlier. Then his eyes began to fill with tears.

'However much we think we're prepared for such times', he whispered, 'it is much, much worse. The pain's terrible. I'm just glad I didn't go before she did – I wouldn't have wanted her to experience such pain.'

By then, I was holding his hand tightly. Still with tears in his eyes, he told me how his wife had battled cancer for sixteen years and also about how good it was that they had those extra years together. My heart went out to him – what more could I say? We were in a secular setting and I knew nothing else about him.

In the end, after asking his name, I told him how my husband and I have been in church ministry for a long time and that I would pray for him. I was unsure how he would react but, in an instant, his face lit up with a lovely, grateful smile and he squeezed my hand. In any other setting, I would have prayed out loud for him then and there but had to be content with a quick, silent prayer instead.

On Encouragement and Comfort

A little later, we chatted briefly again and, when he saw how some of my slides featured scenes from various ruins in Turkey, he told me he had been a tiler and potter. This gave me the opportunity to refer to him as I eventually presented my talk and he smiled and nodded when I did so. Afterwards, I had no chance to chat with him again. But I hoped he had enjoyed my presentation and that both it and the interaction we had had went some small way towards comforting him in his obvious loneliness and grief.

We do not have to look far to find lonely people around us. Some may also be carrying heavy burdens of grief like this man – a grief that needs to be shared and listened to with empathy. From time to time, I continue to pray that this man will have family and friends around him who understand and have time to listen. But, above all, I pray he will experience God's deep comfort in his own latter years and know too that he is never truly alone with God by his side.

I, even I, am he who comforts you.

Isaiah 51:12a

Blessed are those who mourn,
    for they will be comforted.

Matthew 5:4

May we experience the truth of these words too when we walk through dark times. May we know God is with us, holding us close and giving us the strength to stand firm, whatever may happen.

On Encouragement and Comfort

Expect Change

It is not often that I notice billboards beside the road as I drive around our busy city. I am usually too preoccupied keeping my eye on more pressing matters such as speed limits, where I am going or other cars on the road. But one day, a large advertisement on an overpass above the freeway managed to capture my attention. It said very little really – just two words in bold letters: 'EXPECT CHANGE.'

Yes, this ad made me curious as to what sort of changes I might find when shopping in the particular chain of stores it was promoting. But it also caused me to wonder if I needed to apply the same message to my own life in general. You see, I am sure I could be called the archetypal 'glass half-empty' person most of the time. I can usually envisage all sorts of excellent possibilities in some new idea or fresh venture but I am also good at seeing all the potential disasters and difficulties that may occur along the way. This might be a good characteristic to have at times but it can also make one fearful about the future and reluctant to change. In more extreme circumstances, it can even lead to hopelessness and depression.

Yet life is all about change – and the Christian life even more so. After all, it begins with the most radical change ever, as Jesus once explained to Nicodemus:

Very truly I tell you, no one can see the kingdom of God unless they are born again.

John 3:3

We can expect it to continue in the same vein too, since we are urged several times in Scripture to keep growing in God. In 1 Peter 2:2, for example,

On Change

Peter encourages us to be like newborn babies who long for pure spiritual milk in order to grow up in our salvation.

We also need to remember that we belong to a God with whom nothing is impossible – a God who is all-powerful, all-knowing, a God who hears and answers prayer, a God whose heart is the same towards us today as it was towards God's people way back in Jeremiah's time:

'For I know the plans I have for you,' declares the Lord, 'plans to prosper you and not to harm you, plans to give you hope and a future.'

Jeremiah 29:11

With God on our side, we can *expect* things to change – and that change will be for our good. God knows what lies ahead and will guide and strengthen us as we step out with courage and in complete trust and reliance on our amazing God.

Around the same time that I noticed the ad warning me to expect change, I came across a simple question Jesus asked his disciples at one stage: 'However, when the Son of Man comes, will he find faith on the earth?' (Luke 18:8b). While my personality might lead me to weigh things up carefully and see the negatives as well as the positives of any endeavour, I certainly still want Jesus to find me full of faith when he comes. I want to be someone who is hopeful and expectant, up for any changes God might want to make in my life and ready to move as God leads – and I hope you want that too.

On Change

Mustard Seed Moments

'Savour the moment,' the little, old nun told me at a time when I was experiencing deep sadness, 'because you might not pass this way again.'

Our paths crossed only once at a conference. Yet, the more I thought about her words, the more I realised what a gift they were to me. In essence, she encouraged me not to miss out on what God had to teach me right in the midst of that difficult time. I had been given a unique opportunity to experience more of God's love and grace, to grow in my relationship with God and to learn some important lessons about myself – and I needed to grasp it fully.

'That's not humility. That's self-protection,' an insightful pastor told me once at a different stage in my life when I refused to consider a new role in our church that he felt was right for me.

I was shocked but I trusted him and knew he was challenging me in love. I thought I was being humble by pointing out how hopeless I would be in the role. In reality, I panicked and wanted to protect myself from humiliating failure rather than allowing God to help me grow and use me in a different way to bless others. Instead, I needed to rethink my response and rise to the challenge.

'They might not be able to *have* you,' my dear spiritual mentor told me some years later when I wondered whether I was truly wanted in the leadership role I had at church.

On Change

Again, I was shocked. In fact, I found her words quite amusing. Imagine thinking *that* about my situation. The privilege was all mine, wasn't it? Surely, I could not choose to go elsewhere and do something different? Yet I respected my friend and tucked her comment away in my mind to consider at a later date. When that date eventually arrived, I realised what little sense of self-worth I had had for so long and how blind I had been to the work of God's love and grace in my life.

In Matthew's Gospel, we find one of the shortest parables Jesus ever told:

The kingdom of heaven is like a mustard seed, which a man took and planted in his field. Though it is the smallest of all seeds, yet when it grows, it is the largest of garden plants and becomes a tree, so that the birds come and perch in its branches.

Matthew 13:31–2

So many times, God has given me precious, mustard seed moments when one small comment has ended up changing the course of my life in some significant area. With each one, God has shown me a better way to respond to my circumstances or a healthier and more courageous attitude to take on board. Those few brief words I heard enlarged my heart, leaving more room for God, and challenged me just as I needed – and some have also impacted others as I have shared them, face to face or in written form. God has been at work, building the kingdom in me and in others, little by little, word by word.

May we not downplay those tiny mustard seed moments but, instead, notice what God is saying through them and act on them. When we do, the possibilities are infinite.

On Change

Changing the World

It is not often I am challenged on my way *into* church on a Sunday – but, as I discovered not long ago, it can indeed happen. After one of our ministers greeted me that particular morning, we had a brief conversation which, rightly or wrongly, stayed in my mind throughout the service that followed.

In the few moments we had, we talked about how amazing our brains are, in that we can be fully engaged in one activity yet still take in something else happening at the same time. I had commented to him how, on occasions, I have found myself speaking somewhere from the heart on an important topic even while another part of my brain is busily occupied in thinking of practical details that have nothing to do with what I am sharing. I can be fully in the moment, trying to connect on a deep level with those present, yet my mind can simultaneously be busy on another parallel track as well. For example, in mid-sentence, I may find myself noting how someone is smiling or looking upset – or, worse still, bored. Or I might realise I am taking too long with my input and begin thinking about what I need to leave out. Or part of my brain might even be sending me urgent, negative messages such as 'This isn't making sense – it's rubbish. You're making a fool of yourself.' If I then notice someone walk out soon after, these doubts are quickly confirmed.

The profound question my minister friend then asked, however, was this: 'What if we applied *all* of our mind to whatever we were attempting to do, particularly speaking? What would the results be then?'

Much as I hate to admit it, my immediate response was, 'Oh, we might change the world!' It was not so much *what* I said but the flippant way I said

On Change

it that makes me shudder now. I say that because, the more I reflected on my response, the more I realised that, if our minds were totally filled with God's message for those present and totally filled with the Spirit of God as we spoke, then I believe it is entirely possible we *could* change the world by the power of God.

In the same church service, we were reminded of the following words of Jesus:

All authority in heaven and on earth has been given to me. Therefore go and make disciples of all nations, baptising them in the name of the Father and of the Son and of the Holy Spirit, and teaching them to obey everything I have commanded you. And surely I am with you always, to the very end of the age.
Matthew 28:18-20

Maybe then it would be better if, next time I speak, I focus fully on the One who is with me forever, the One who has *all* authority and can very well deal with any of my extraneous thoughts. It would certainly be better if I were to shut out the destructive, negative messages from the enemy that tend to invade my brain and, instead, listen more carefully to God's loving, positive, empowering words.

With all my heart, I want to be part of changing our world as God guides and empowers. May that be your sincere heart's desire too.

On Change

Walking Away from the Offer of a Lifetime

I wonder if you can recall a time when you decided against pursuing a particular career or course of study or when you perhaps closed the door on one part of your life and opted to head in a different direction. How did you feel as you made such a key decision?

I still remember the moment I turned my back on high-school teaching in the late eighties and took up an editing job instead. Part of me was relieved, but another part was sorry to walk away from the classroom setting and the opportunity to engage with so many young people. I can well remember my sorrow at resigning from a ministry position a few years later too, even after initially agreeing to stay for a further four years. I knew God had something else for me to do, which turned out to be writing and speaking, but I hated disappointing our church and walking away from a role I loved.

These decisions, however, pale in comparison to the one made by the rich, young man we read about in Mark 10. Jesus gives this man the offer of a lifetime, in answer to his question about how to inherit eternal life: '"One thing you lack," he said. "Go, sell everything you have and give to the poor, and you will have treasure in heaven. Then come, follow me"' (verse 21b).

It is not as if Jesus says this harshly at all. In the first part of this verse, we see how much he cares for this young man and longs for him to make the right decision: 'Jesus looked at him and loved him' (verse 21a). What beautiful words – so simple, yet so profound. As you read them, can you imagine yourself in this scene, either as an onlooker or even as the rich, young man himself?

On Change

I chose to do the latter. I imagined myself coming to Jesus with a sincere question about eternal life. I listened as Jesus responded and I answered him honestly. At that point, I could not believe my eyes and ears. Jesus was standing there, looking straight at me with such love – and my heart almost turned over. But his words were too much for me. I wanted to follow him with all my heart, yet all the beautiful things I own flashed before my eyes and I wanted them so much too. I turned away from his loving eyes – but, even as I did, my heart felt so, so heavy.

I am not this young man. But this whole experience of allowing Jesus' words to come alive in a fresh way for me left me with some key questions to answer. What holds me back from following Jesus with all my heart each day? Are there areas in my life where I still turn from him and go my own way, unwilling to give everything in response to his love for me? Have I forgotten those eyes of love with which Jesus looks at me each day, just as he looked at that rich, young man so long ago?

May we not walk away from the amazing, life-giving offer Jesus extends to each one of us. Instead, may we look him full in the face, listen – and do as he says.

On Change

Seeing with Fresh Eyes

One day during the school holidays, we decided to take our two youngest grandchildren to a new zoo, courtesy of some discount vouchers. At first, our grandson wanted to head straight for the crocodiles, but we persuaded him not to ignore the other animals nearby, starting with the cute, little meerkats. Then we managed to arrive at the elephant enclosure exactly on feeding time. After the zoo-keeper had asked the crowd a couple of questions, she chose our grandson to answer them since his hand had shot up so quickly. I held my breath – and, to my amazement, both his answers were correct.

'How did you know all that?' I asked him.

'I read on the sign back there how African elephants have bigger ears than Asian ones,' he told me, 'and I just guessed elephants don't have any bones in their trunks!'

He was alert and definitely engaged. As we kept walking, I began to see all the animals with fresh eyes – the eyes of a 9-year-old boy and his 7-year-old sister. We did our best to spot the African painted dog and the sleepy hyenas. We marvelled at the size of the giraffes, the lion and the weird-looking camels. We watched fascinated as the elegant tiger prowled straight towards its 'prey', a cardboard, cut-out zebra in which the keepers had hidden its food. Then at last, we reached the huge, scary-looking crocodile in its tank. Both children watched entranced for ages as it slowly moved towards the surface, much to their joy. They were definitely impressed with that crocodile, and soon I too began to marvel at its amazing ridged, armour-like skin, large claws and, of course, those menacing, razor-sharp teeth.

On Change

Not long after, we reached the reptile house where the huge pythons we discovered there almost eclipsed the crocodile, along with gaudy, green tree snakes and large lizards, some so well camouflaged that I needed our grandchildren's help to spot them. Then, of all things, the frogs captured our granddaughter's attention. Yes, I was definitely seeing these more ordinary little creatures with fresh eyes too.

As I reflected on our zoo experiences, I began to wonder what else in my life I needed to look at with fresh eyes – perhaps even with the eyes of a child. What about the trees outside my window and the beautiful flowering shrubs nearby? Had I lost some of the awe and wonder I once felt when gazing at God's handiwork around me in nature? What about my family and friends? Had I failed lately to appreciate aspects of God's image in those closest to me? But above all, what about our amazing Creator God? Did I also need to open my eyes, take a fresh look at what God has done in my own life and be much more thankful for it all?

I remembered then the words and actions of Jesus on one occasion:

He called a little child to him, and placed the child among them. And he said: "Truly I tell you, unless you change and become like little children, you will never enter the kingdom of heaven".

Matthew 18:2–3

May we all be open to seeing God with fresh eyes, humble enough to change and ready to cultivate a childlike heart that looks, marvels and truly believes.

On Change

Something to Live For

How would you respond if someone asked you what you live for right now? It can be a confronting question – and perhaps our response might vary according to who is asking, how honest we want to be and also our overall level of health and wellbeing.

Recently, I talked with someone in her nineties after a meeting where she had tried to inspire others to continue running a group she had begun over twenty years earlier. I felt sorry for her because there seemed to be no one to take up the challenge, and I admired her fighting spirit to keep pursuing her goal, despite ill health and old age. But I wondered too why she still cared so much about it all, to the point of worrying over it day and night.

As we left, I tried to calm her down as best I could. 'Don't worry,' I told her. 'I'm sure it will work out. Be at peace.'

She looked doubtful, then responded in a way that made me feel even more sorry for her.

'Well, I hope it does. I need something to live for.'

Sometime later, I thoughtlessly mentioned this conversation to someone else who has serious health issues. They did not respond, but I could see the look of understanding in their eyes and glimpsed their own longing to be able to continue contributing to our world in a meaningful way. My heart went out to this person too – and I wondered how I would feel and respond in a similar situation.

On Change

There seems to be an inbuilt desire in most of us to *matter* in some way to others in life – or to some significant other at least – and to know there is a purpose to our being here on this earth. Yet there are so many factors in life that we cannot control, aren't there? In the end, we cannot *make* people accept and value us or our contribution to society. They may well prefer others and what they offer over who we are and what we can do. It is wonderful when we receive the love and affirmation that we feel we need from others, but when this is no longer available to us for whatever reason, it is so important to have our own inner resources in place that give meaning to life and enable us to press on and continue to have hope.

Surely this is where knowing the love and grace of God and experiencing deep in our hearts how much God values and fully accepts each one of us is so important. Others may not understand or value us, but God always will. Others may fail us, but God never will. Our minds and bodies may crumble, but God never changes and will be there forever.

For me, belonging to God makes all the difference. Whatever happens, I know God is with me and has a purpose for my life. The outworking of this purpose may change over time, but I can be at peace, knowing God has my back and is in control.

I hope those two people I spoke with know this for themselves – and I hope you do too.

I have loved you with an everlasting love.

Jeremiah 31:3a

Never will I leave you;
never will I forsake you.

Hebrews 13:5b

On Change

The Best Invitation

What fun we had some years ago as we prepared to move house. In every room, there were piles of boxes filled with photo albums, music, pictures, board games and other paraphernalia – not to mention books, books and more books. Outside, our recycling bin was also filled to capacity with old files, books no one else would want to read and music very few would want to sing or play now.

I suspect my husband's part in all this was more challenging than mine. You see, he had a whole wall of built-in shelves in his study, brimful of old books that needed to be culled severely. But perhaps the hardest task of all for him was dispensing with bulging folders of notes from courses he had undertaken for his Doctor of Ministry studies, along with his resulting three-volume dissertation.

'I feel I'm throwing a key part of my life away,' he commented sadly one day.

I understood his sense of loss, to some degree at least. I too dispensed with many folders containing courses I had helped devise and run, manuals from various other programmes I had attended, as well as many sermon notes. It was difficult at times but, in the end, we found several ways of approaching this culling and packing adventure that prevented us from become too overwhelmed by it all.

First, we realised the importance of acknowledging any grief we felt as we threw out work that represented a significant part of our lives or personal growth experiences. Yes, we had put our whole selves into preparing this or that course or set of lectures. Yes, those days were gone. But we soon

On Change

realised God was right there with us in the midst of it all, bringing comfort and also whispering a gentle 'Well done, good and faithful servant' into our hearts.

Second, while not ignoring any sense of loss we felt, we tried to adopt a more positive attitude. We decided to thank God for the variety of opportunities we have been afforded in our lives to learn about so many things and to serve others by sharing our knowledge with them. We remembered how fulfilling it was to use our gifts in these ways and how others grew closer to God as a result. How privileged we had been to be entrusted with such tasks in God's kingdom.

But perhaps the most helpful approach to all this culling before our impending move came via an insightful question a friend asked me one day: 'So . . . what is the invitation God is extending to you for the next part of your life?'

What a beautiful thought! Why would we keep looking back when we could turn around and accept God's gracious invitation to move forward into the next part of our life? After all, God knows us and loves us – and still has a myriad of ways for us to bless others in the future. We were not finished with everything for good.

May you too reach that same conclusion and step into the rest of your life with deep joy and confidence in God.

Trust in the Lord with all your heart
    and lean not on your own understanding;
in all your ways submit to him,
    and he will make your paths straight.

Proverbs 3:5–6

On Change

Jo-Anne Berthelsen

Jo-Anne Berthelsen lives in Sydney, Australia, and is the author of seven published novels and four non-fiction books. She holds degrees in arts and theology and has worked in teaching, editing and local church ministry. Jo-Anne loves encouraging others through both the written and spoken word and is a keen blogger.

www.jo-anneberthelsen.com
www.joanneberthelsen.wordpress.com

Notes

Moment 3

[1]   Anna B. Warner (1860) and William B. Bradbury (1862), Public domain.

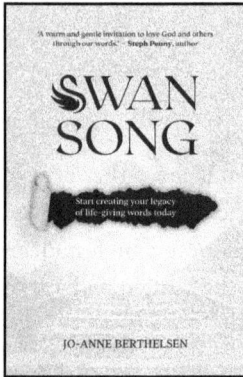

Swansong

*Start creating your legacy of
life-giving words today*

Jo-Anne Berthelsen

Do we want to be known as someone who builds others up or tears
them down?

The words we speak to each other have real impact. They can bring
love and acceptance, but they can also hurt and destroy.

Jo-Anne Berthelsen encourages us to make our interactions with others as positive as we can through God's strength. Combining her own
experiences with biblical teaching, Jo-Anne shares how twelve words
including empathy, affirmation and forgiveness can be used to build
up those around us.

By being more intentional about the way we speak on a daily basis,
we can create our own unique legacy of life-giving words that reveals
God's heart to those around us.

978-1-78893-339-1

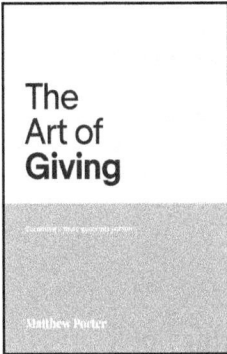

The Art of Giving

Becoming a more generous person

Matthew Porter

978-1-78893-290-5

The Art of Journalling

Becoming a more reflective person

Matthew Porter

978-1-78893-288-2

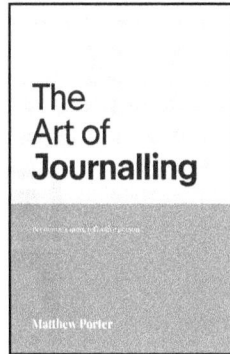

The Art of … is a series of books about discipleship habits.

In each book a spiritual habit is explained and explored in an accessible way, and you are encouraged to practise this art through practical pointers and exercises. By developing these holy habits, you can become a more fruitful and fulfilled missional disciple of Jesus.

Authentic

We trust you enjoyed reading this book from Authentic. If you want to be informed of any new titles from this author and other releases you can sign up to the Authentic newsletter by scanning below:

Online:
authenticmedia.co.uk

Follow us: